MW00831590

Praise for *Brief Hours and Weeks:*
My Life as a Capetonian

"What a delight. It succeeds in writerly craft, narrative, evocation of people, times and places and—not least—in authorial courage and candor."
— James Grant,
author of *Bagehot: The Life and Times of the Greatest Victorian*

"This is a touching, evocative (and beautifully illustrated) memoir, a vibrant portrayal of a vanished yet not wholly distant world. Emanuel Derman paints a convincing picture with great skill, candour and humanity. These are precious memories, which you will enjoy reading."
— Stefan Stern,
former *Financial Times* columnist and author

"Professor Derman writes with such honesty, openness and detail that I feel I may have developed false memories. 'But, Paul, you aren't Jewish and you've never been to Cape Town.' Now I'm not so sure."
— Paul Wilmott, mathematician, author and semi-professional controversialist

Praise for *My Life as a Quant*

"Derman's memoir of his transition from mathematical physicist to expert finance whiz at Goldman Sachs and Salomon Brothers reads like a novel, but tells a lot about brains applied to making money grow."
> —Paul A. Samuelson, MIT, Nobel Laureate in Economic Sciences, 1970

"*My Life as a Quant*, by Emanuel Derman, is, indeed, a perfect memoir, as Derman, a South African–born physicist turned financial engineer, is a perfect memoirist."
> —*Grant's Interest Rate Observer*

"There are few 'gentlemen bankers' left these days. Nor is there much room in the great financial houses for anything that smacks of the amateur spirit. That is why Emanuel Derman's memoirs are so compelling...Derman's wry humour and sense of irony are apparent throughout the book."
> —*Financial Times*

"That sense of being an intruder in outlaw territory lends an intriguing mood to Derman's *My Life as a Quant*, a literate and entertaining memoir."
> —*Business Week*

Also by Emanuel Derman

My Life as a Quant: Reflections on Physics and Finance
Models.Behaving.Badly

Brief Hours and Weeks: My Life as a Capetonian
©Emanuel Derman, 2024
The LML Press
ISBN 978-1-0686491-0-3 (hardback)
ISBN 978-1-0686491-1-0 (ebook)

BRIEF HOURS AND WEEKS:
MY LIFE AS A CAPETONIAN
EMANUEL DERMAN

The LML Press
London
Publisher of the London Mathematical Laboratory
lmlpress.org.uk

There are three kinds of people:
interesting people, boring people, and people you love.

Contents

Chapter 1.
Separation Anxiety
How can one have everything?

In daylight, a dark curtained room filled with a dark dining table. Several doors lead off it. I want to go through one of them to a bedroom on the far side but they won't let me. It must have been when we still lived on Burns Road and my father's mother, Henye Leah Dereczynski, had died, and her body was lying in that bedroom. It is 1946 and I am thirteen months old.

That was the dining table my sister Ruth was made to lie down on when they anaesthetised her and removed her tonsils. The big things happened at home in those days.

My mother's best friend, Mrs Schwartz, saved my life when I was a few weeks old. With bronchitis, a blocked nose, and a cough, I couldn't take my mother's breast. It was Mrs Schwartz, my mother says, who persisted, who encouraged my mother, who fed me with a teaspoon. So here I am.

My mother tells me later that she went to the doctor when she thought she might be pregnant at age thirty-nine. "What will I do now?" she exclaimed when he confirmed it, confirming in turn that I am an error.

 Now we live on Victoria Road, the main throughway of our poor mixed-race neighbourhood of Salt River. My father owns a nearby garage, Union Service Station, that has Atlantic-Petrol-branded pumps in front of it. His garage is on Salt River Road, which runs perpendicularly from Victoria Road down to Lower Main Road, where the Schwartzes own a dress shop.

The Schwartzes and my parents are *landsleit*, immigrants from the same region of Poland to "Cup-peh To-ven," as my mother imagined that "Cape Town" was pronounced in Polish, when she first heard about the possibility of going there in 1933. Now they are Capetonians and they go to bioscope together on Saturday nights. But some old-world formality persists: they never use each other's first names. My mother always addresses them in conversation as Mr or Mrs Schwartz, and they call her Mrs Derman.

She has me when she is forty, nine years after my sister Ruth is born in Cape Town and twelve years after my sister Shulamit is born in Poland. She works every day in my father's garage, pumping petrol and making him Nescafe and toasted cheese sandwiches at lunchtime in his small office. A rich man, she tells us once half-amusedly, the father of a school friend we all know, had invited her to take a ride with him when she finished filling his car.

I miss her when she is away at work. I sit on the front steps of the stoop of our house, looking down in the direction of the garage around the corner, and try to reel her in with my imaginary fishing rod, winding the imaginary spool. I know it won't work but I like doing it.

When she is at home on Victoria Road she can pick up the receiver of the wall phone just inside the front door of our house, turn a crank on its side that goes *brrr brrr brrr*, and have it ring in the garage to reach my father directly. One block below the garage, on the next corner, is a little Indian shop, Miyan's, where my father takes me to buy sweets. Ruth says he used to take her there too, every Saturday morning, and then to the library to borrow a book. The shop is still there more than 75 years later.

Despite owning a garage, my father never learns to drive. When we get our first car, a navy 1948 Chevrolet, license CA 61274, my mother is the one who learns to drive and remains the only driver, until my sisters learn, and then me. There is a photo of my father, my mother, my sister Ruth and me, standing to the side of our new car in front of my father's garage. It's my father who has me protectively beside him rather than my mother.

IT'S THE WOMEN WHO COMFORT ME

Ruth wheels me around the block in my pram in the morning before she goes to school.

Half a pound of tuppeny rice
Half a pound of treacle
Mix them up and make them nice
Pop goes the weasel!

On the final line she gives the pram a big jerk, a ritual of expected and longed-for fear and excitement. I do this later with my kids and grandkids.

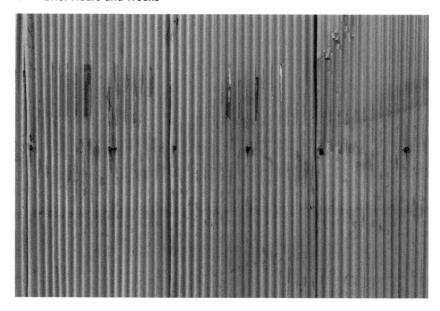

Marie, the Coloured[1] maid who lives with us, looks after me when my mother is away. She has her own son, Joseph, older than me, who sometimes lives with us too, and a mother called Sophie.[2] Marie takes me for a walk beside the park. I have just had my fingernails cut, and I run my newly bare fingertips over the sinusoidal bump bump bump of the dusty green corrugated iron fence. It's a strange pleasurable sensation to have the now raw ends of my fingers bounce and throb over the metal. My fingers turn a little green and grey from the dust. Marie quickly scolds me for getting my hands dirty and wipes them clean. She is too strict with me. My sisters want her to let me be more of a boy instead of a flower-smeller.

Marie looks after me a lot. She is let go soon, perhaps for stealing, and I'm told years later that I missed her, though I don't remember that part nor who came after her. Did her strictness and her early disappearance affect my character, add to my anxiety?

1 Coloured is the commonly accepted name of a racial group in the Cape Province of South Africa. This book is about a time and place now gone, seen through the eyes and lips of someone growing up then.

2 Live-in maids, who are often single mothers and cook and clean and look after families' kids, frequently send their own kids back to the country town they came from, to be brought up by their more distant relatives.

When my parents go to bioscope in town on a Saturday night, I often wake up before they come home and cry for my mother. Ruth sings me a song she made up, one with infinite verses:

Mommy and Daddy are leaving the film, coming home to
Emanuel;
Mommy and Daddy are walking to the car, coming home to
Emanuel;
Mommy and Daddy are starting the car, ready to come to
Emanuel;
Mommy and Daddy are driving back home, coming home to
Emanuel;
Mommy and Daddy are stopping at the shop, to buy sweets for
Emanuel;
Mommy and Daddy are driving again, on their way home to
Emanuel;
...

and so she continues until I fall asleep, or they arrive.

When I wake in the middle of the night or early morning I call for my father who comes to lift me up and take me to sleep in their bed, two single beds pushed together. I like to lie cuddled in the groove between them, but I want to have my feet on my mother's side.

IT'S MY FATHER WHO PLAYS WITH ME

 I don't think my mother ever entertains me. My father carries me on his back, tells me Bible stories. At bedtime I am allowed to choose the long version or the short version. He plays *putch* (Yiddish for "slap"), in which he rests his hands on mine and I try to flip my hands and slap his before he can remove them. He encourages me to sing. He lets me pretend to be a doctor and examine him. I still have a miniature 78 rpm record, recorded in a kiosk on the English-style boardwalk in the seaside resort of Muizenberg, a South-African-Jewish Blackpool. He takes me into the little booth and has me sing Hebrew songs which the kiosk proprietor records with a needle in a long engraved spiral on a small dark brown vinyl-coated tin plate. I am singing serious stuff, *The WWII Jewish Partisan's Song* in Hebrew, and *Kshenamut*, a tuneful Zionist plea to be buried in the wine cellars of Rishon LeZion when we die. My father, in his heavy foreign accent that embarrasses me throughout my childhood, can be heard periodically prompting me on the vinyl when I hesitate in the middle of a song. Some days he takes me into the *camera obscura* on the elevated promenade above the beach where, in the dim darkness, you see projected on the table the moving images of people strolling outside.

There is a photo of him and me on the beach. I am two years old, barefoot in a short-sleeved shirt, chortling at whoever is taking the photo. My father has a weak reluctant smile and is wearing a suit – trousers and a jacket – to walk on the sand, with a V-neck sweater over his shirt. Why is he dressed that way?

My first recollection of being embarrassed by my father is a few years later, when he carries me on his back around the beach, and I see another boy from kindergarten nearby. I am too old for this. I bury my face in my father's back, pretending I don't see the boy.

My father calls me by his own affectionate diminutives, *Emanuel-ke*, sometimes even *Bok-kele*, the Yiddish word for a little goat.[3] Since he had all his remaining bad teeth pulled at age fifty and thinks that's normal, and since he wants to make me happy, he gives me eight squares of Nestlé chocolate to eat in bed at night while I look at books. He says that if I eat a bit of apple afterwards it will cancel out the effect of the chocolate. It doesn't, and so at age twelve I get gold foil fillings in my front teeth.[4]

He must have loved me more than I realised, and I him. He must have been very sad when I left and never came back to live there. But in your prime you don't think about such things.

---

3 I had always thought *Bok-kele* meant a little deer, until I looked it up. A little goat doesn't sound that lovable.

4 No one makes these anymore. Dentists used to create the filling by forcing thin sheets of gold foil, layer by layer, into the cavity until they cold-welded together. They apparently fit cavities extremely well because of the incremental construction. They last many decades and mine are admired by New York dentists as a lost art.

LIKES, NEEDS, FEARS AND GUILTS

I like girls, unlike my cousin Leopold who, everyone knows, will fly into a fist-fighting fury if an adult teases him by saying he likes a girl. There's a photo of me kissing Sharon, the daughter of our neighbour, on the walkway of our Salt River house. Later, when I have seen some films, I like to show off by demonstrating a "film kiss" of the 1950s that involves pressing my closed mouth for a long time against my mother's.

I am notorious in the extended family for being spoiled, a "bad eater"[5]. I hate the taste of milk and especially the skin that forms on it. I hate soft-boiled eggs – they might make me vomit.[6] I will reliably eat only lamb chops and chips. I like toasted cheese sandwiches, which you can buy only in restaurants. But my mother ingeniously figures out that she can make them by wrapping a cheese

---

[5] My mother has friends from Pretoria, the Reitziks, who knew her back in Poland, and they will not tolerate bad eaters. When their twins were small, they sent them away to live with a bad-eater-fixer family who, by repeatedly putting the uneaten food back in front of the twins at the next meal, taught them to become good eaters.

[6] As Doris Lessing writes in *Under My Skin*: "A small child does not taste anything like the same omelette an adult does ... Smells expand the nose in delight, shrivel it in disgust ... Children and adults do not live in the same sensory world."

sandwich in waxed paper, covering it with a dish towel, and then pressing it repeatedly with a hot clothes iron. She buys an extra iron and keeps it in my father's office at the garage so she can make them for him at lunchtime. When I visit my cousin Abner, whose family lives a few blocks away on Roodebloem Road, I ask for a toasted cheese sandwich. When my aunt Chayele says she doesn't have a toasted cheese maker, I proudly explain to her how to do it. A few years later I also proudly show Chayele how I can read and pronounce Yiddish written in Hebrew characters.

I like to sit on the front steps of our house, facing the street. One afternoon an old bearded *bergie* leans over the gate and speaks to me. I get scared and run inside for safety. When my mother and sisters comfort me, I feel guilty for having hurt his feelings.

All my life I feel a bit like an outsider, and I like that feeling.

I sit on the steps in the afternoons after returning from kindergarten and hold a rectangular mirror in my hands, adjusting it to aim the reflected sunlight onto the interior walls and counters and people in the Portuguese fish-and-chip shop across Victoria Road. I like to dazzle them. The Portuguese lady who runs it comes to our house to complain to my mother.

In the living room one afternoon, I sit on the floor and listen to the wireless. It's a show about Jesus that is strangely persuasive, but I know I am Jewish and that this isn't right.

I am scared of having my photo taken: I think I will disappear into the camera.

I am scared of having my long hair cut: my mother takes me to town to the barber where my cousin Leopold has his hair cut while sitting alone in the big black chair. My mother lets me sit on her lap while the barber trims it.

I am four, and I like to play with the garden hose in front of our house. I stand on the red cement walkway that runs from the front gate to the front door and grip the rubber hose, aiming it so that the shiny brass nozzle's parabola of water lands on the little lawn on the right. Then I want to make the water go to the little lawn on the left. I swing the black rubber snake with both fists, aiming to make the stream leap through the air without any water touching the cement. The nozzle strikes the forehead of my father who has come up behind me. He is taken to the hospital for stitches. I know it's my fault.

On a family outing to The Gay Adventure ice cream parlour in Lakeside I am greedy and insist on two helpings of ice cream before eating one, and then cannot eat the second. After that, Ruth periodically teases me: Remember the ice cream at The Gay Adventure! And I am periodically shown the print we have at home of a little boy with two pieces of cake, one in each hand, looking perplexed and saying "If only I had two moufs!" Their teasing rankles. I remember it.

"If only I had two moufs!"

Perhaps they see something in me that I am not yet aware of, a wanting more than is possible and imagining I can have it, an inability to compromise. Later in life I have the deluded feeling that I have no limits, that I can be better than anybody at almost anything, by natural ability. (I could probably be a really good miler!) Perhaps I have been overly praised?

There are so many dichotomies: pleasing oneself vs. pleasing others, growing up vs. staying a child, the independence of loneliness vs. the comfort of the group, domesticity vs. excitement, dangerous eroticism vs. duller safety. How can one have everything?

Chapter 2
Prost or Eidel

*My mother's mysteriously glamorous past • Are we eidel or
prost? • Yiddish curses*

My mother's name in Cape Town is Sonia. She was Sara Sapirsz-
tejnówna in Polish, Chaye Sara in Yiddish or Hebrew. In school,
other girls teased her by chanting *Mała Żydówka Chayka gra na
bałałajce* (Little Jewess Chayka Plays the Balalaika). She has no
blood relatives in Cape Town other than us children. On principle,
her principle, she gives all of us names that will be identical in English and Hebrew, so we are Shulamit, Ruth, and Emanuel. None
of us have middle names.

My father's name is Chaim in any country or language, stubbornly the same in English, Polish, and Hebrew, as I see on my
parents' wedding certificate and on his tombstone.

Some of his gentile business associates who know only English pronounce it "Chame," rhyming with "shame" but with a hard initial "ch," as in "chapter." He never stoops to anglicise it to Hyman or Charles, and is proud of that.

HER PAST IS A MYSTERY TO ME

In 1955, on my mother's fiftieth birthday, when I was almost ten years old, our teacher began the day as usual by writing the date on the blackboard: 05.05.55. It was only later that I realised the perfection of my mother's birthdate: 05.05.05.

She was born in Ružany, Poland, a town of perhaps 10,000, now in the Brest district of Belarus. She was the eldest of the six children of Nahum Zvi and Rivka Sapirstein. When she was a little girl, they ambitiously sent her away from home to attend school in Brest Litovsk, a much larger town. She boarded with strangers and cried herself to sleep at night but didn't let anyone know so as not to upset her parents. This was her lifelong theme, stoicism, or perhaps a sadness that had to be kept secret. Later, her whole family moved to Brest Litovsk.

Perhaps because of her childhood, she teaches me to mollify people. "*Alemen darf a glet*," she likes to say in Yiddish. *Everyone needs a caress.*

My mother was very beautiful when she was young, more so than anyone in her family and much more so than anyone in my father's. She married late, at almost twenty-seven. It wasn't an arranged marriage, but since they lived in different towns, someone must have introduced them with a purpose.

They look mismatched in their wedding photo – she Greta Gar-
bo-ish and sophisticatedly European-looking, he seated, earnest
and boyish and slightly naive-looking. The woman in that photo is
not at all the mother I knew. The man is more like my father than
she is like my mother.

Her past is a mystery to me and her youth especially so. How
did she undergo this metamorphosis from film star to immigrant,
hard-labouring mother, and housewife? Who introduced her to my
father in Slonim when she lived in Brest Litovsk? Why did she marry so late? What did she do during the almost ten years between
finishing high school in Brest Litovsk and getting married? She
may have worked for her father, a bookkeeper. My sister Shulamit
used to say my mother had been in love with a man in Brest whom
her parents didn't approve of because he came from the wrong side
of the tracks.

In her wardrobe my mother has one shoe box of the past, in it
a small number of Yiddish letters and other mementos of her parents that she brought to Cape Town. When she gets older she talks
about tearing the letters up because no one will read them when
she is gone. She has no photos from that time except for one of her
two youngest siblings who were left behind in the Holocaust. She
doesn't talk about that.

My parents married in Slonim in 1932. After the birth of Shulamit in 1933 my father left for Cape Town to join his mother, brothers, and sister and carry out reconnaissance for the future; meanwhile, my mother and Shulamit went back to live with her parents in Brest. It's hard for me to picture it but Shulamit believed my mother enjoyed her social life during those two years in Brest after my father left – a single mother with grandparents to look after the baby and no need to work hard. Two years later they followed, sailing to Cape Town, perhaps via England or Italy. Then the immigrant struggle began. Still, better than ending up in a concentration camp.

My mother has three standards that rule her life: family, stoicism, and *eidelkeit*.

FAMILY

Family means children. The mother of one of my friends, Mrs K, told my mother: "My husband is more important than my children." My mother repeated this statement to us incredulously several times. It was incomprehensible to her. And Mrs Wilken, the recently widowed and childless middle-aged Afrikaner lady next door, told my mother across the fence that separated our houses that she had met a man in her church and was in love with him. That, too, was inconceivable to my mother, quite laughable; Mrs Wilken had lost her mind. My mother could better understand the wife of our school Hebrew teacher, who said of her husband and children: *He's just the man I married, but they are my flesh and blood.*

STOICISM

She has suffered many losses and does not complain. Besides Shulamit, Ruth, and me, the only blood relatives she has left in the world are in Israel: two younger sisters, Naomi and Yafa, and a younger brother, Yossel. The three of them jointly emigrated from Poland to Palestine in the early 1930s, when she herself came to Cape Town. She does not see them for the next fifteen years.

Her youngest brother, Leibel, and youngest sister, Paia, had been too young to emigrate when their siblings did and stayed behind in Brest Litovsk with their parents. They all perished together. My mother rarely speaks of them.

 She has one other photo of twelve-year-old Leibel in a short-sleeved polo. Looking at it today makes me sad – he could be a regular 2024 teenage kid you might see in Riverside Park some afternoon. How to imagine him death-camped?

All correspondence from Poland ceased in 1942. The Germans seized the *Brest ghetto* on the first day of Operation Barbarossa against the Soviet Union, and "...Less than a year after the creation of the ghetto, around October 15–18, 1942, most of approximately 20,000 Jewish inhabitants of Brest (Brześć) were murdered." If she'd been certain her father was dead in 1945, my mother would have named me Nahum.

So, from 1935 on, my mother was in Africa, surrounded by a giant family of scores of in-laws who (I later realise) were less genteel than her blood family, now left behind forever. She is the rock of our immediate family and the larger family, too. She stoically supports my father when he gets anxious or depressed, which he does periodically. She works in the garage with him. She spends ages patiently reassuring my aunt Lizzie, an aunt by marriage, who has severe OCD and worries about having harmed her visiting nieces by feeding them the wrong kind of food. Most everyone in our extended family brings their problems, personal and interpersonal, to my mother, but it's not reciprocal. She takes hers mainly to my sisters. She likes wise sayings and collects them from the *Cape Times* "Thought for the Day" feature. She especially likes those of Rabindranath Tagore, partly imagining, I suspect, that the "Rabi" syllables in his name are some secret link to Jewishness. "I cried because I had no shoes until I met a man who had no feet," she often likes to say. In the 1960s she sometimes has dreams when she sleeps in the afternoon, dreams in which she wants to wake up but cannot. She tells me that if I ever hear her struggling in her sleep, I should wake her.

This stoicism stands her in good stead when she comes down with ALS in 1970 and suffers through the next nine years.

EIDELKEIT

More than any other quality, my mother cares about *eidelkeit*, Yiddish for "refinement." She looks down on vulgarity and commonness, as does my father. The worst thing to say about a non-evil person is that they are *prost*, Polish-Yiddish for vulgar. She also looks down on people with insufficient education. But, to be fair, she recognises that uneducated people can be *eidel* too. One can be *eidel* by nature.

We, I deduce from many remarks about others, are *eidel*. Why, I wonder later, is *prost*ness such a big deal to my immigrant parents, such a demarcator of people? Vulgarity is a big deal to my grown sisters too. Is it the *narcissism of small differences* among competitive immigrants? Were we really *eidel*? My sisters believe so, firmly and proudly. My mother, I decide, really was *eidel*. The rest of us, I'm really not sure.

Everybody loves my mother. She is gracious and reserved and attractive and welcoming. Not only extended family members but also my childhood friends come to her with their troubles. She gives them a cup of tea and several of her famous home-baked cupcakes covered with icing and sprinkled with hundreds-and-thousands. What none of them can see is that she herself is wary of people; she holds herself tight. Social life is a strain for her, but that's the life she has to live among strangers.

In my old age, I become a bit like that myself; I don't like parties or large dinners. There are only a few people with whom I'm comfortable enough to spend a large amount of time.[7]

YIDDISH WORDS, ENTREATIES, AND CURSES

My parents speak Yiddish to each other, but often also to us. It's not a language they can use to hide facts or opinions – for that, they must resort to Polish. But their Yiddish is filled with Polish-Yiddish compliments and curses:

Krasavetz – a handsome boy
Krasavetza – a beautiful girl
Drobne – small change
Prichoska – a fancy hairdo, a styled wave in the hair. I hear this a lot when Tony Curtis's forehead curl becomes popular with 1950s teenagers.

Paskudniak – a really despicable, disgusting person, a crook

7 I like to think that there are three kinds of people: interesting people, boring people, and people you love.

Psha-kref! – Dog's blood! (This is, mysteriously, very very bad. When I ask her what it means my mother is embarrassed to have said it. When I push her, she reluctantly explains it meant *hundische blut.*)

A kholera af dir – a cholera on you

A kadoches af dir – a fever on you

Vos willst du vun meine leben? Vos legst du mir in drerd? – What do you want of my life? Why are you putting me in the grave? (This last one is usually directed at spouses or children who cause grief.)

Chapter 3
Coloureds, Whites, Gentiles and Jews

I am much more aware of the difference between Jews and Gentiles than of the difference between whites and Coloureds.

Salt River, where we live from 1945 until mid-1952, is full of Coloureds and whites who intermingle more or less freely in business, housing, and school. The Group Areas Act, which systematised segregation in housing and everything else, became South African law only in 1950 after the Nationalist (mostly Afrikaner) government took power.

My father's chief helper in the Salt River garage is a Coloured man, David. Every weekday morning in 1948 and 1949, he drives my sister Ruth and me from Salt River to Hope St, where Ruth goes to Good Hope Seminary for Girls and I go to kindergarten at the small newly founded Herzlia Day School for Jewish children. Sometimes David drives us there in my mother's car and sometimes in the garage pickup in which he lets me change gears on the stick shift while he pushes down on the clutch pedal. One morning, probably from having eaten an egg, I vomit on Ruth's school shoes and uniform, but she has to make it through the day smelly.

Baigley is another of my father's employees, more of a physical worker than a jack-of-all-trades like David. Late one morning, to amuse me, he takes gunpowder-filled caps from my toy cap gun and layers a pile of them one by one into a metal screw-cap that he had removed from the valve of a tyre, puts it on the black oil-covered floor of the garage, and then hits it as hard as he can with a big sledgehammer. The IED explodes more fiercely than he intends, providing me with not just a gigantic bang but also bits of shrapnel in my eyes, which I shut tightly and refuse to open. They take me to a chemist nearby who puts some glycerine under my lids. No one seems to hold the incident against Baigley, and neither do I.

I like the garage. I like seeing cars go up on the hydraulic lift so that someone can work on them from below. I especially like the smell of petrol, and already know that I will like smoking when I grow up. I like the interference reflection patterns that the spilled oil and water make on the ground all around the garage.

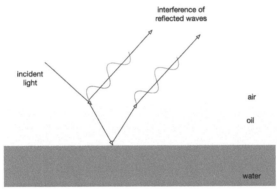

Sick in bed one afternoon in my room in the back of our house, I think I hear our family doctor come in the front door and say something in Yiddish to my parents. I fear doctors' visits. Thankfully it is Mr Jenkins, the Coloured plumber who sounds similar to our doctor and can speak some Yiddish too.

Joseph, the son of our maid[8], Marie, lives with us on occasion. He probably lives away from Cape Town with Marie's relatives, and she works full-time for us. He is older than my second cousin Abner, and more worldly. He has a pocket knife and knows how to make a kite out of two tree branches lashed together with string into a cross and then covered with tissue paper. He knows you need to add a long ribbon tail for stability. One Saturday morning Abner and I want to make one. It is Shabbat, and though we are not ob-

8 Doris Lessing in *Under My Skin* refers to "servants" rather than "maids" or "boys" in 1940's Southern Rhodesia, and I think that we may have used her terminology too. How strange it sounds.

servant, we know we shouldn't be cutting and working on this day. We try to break tree branches accidentally-on-purpose in the right place – accidentally-on-purpose so as not to violate the Sabbath, though we know that accidentally-on-purpose is still a violation. Eventually, we ask knowledgeable Joseph to do the job for us with his knife. We invent the *Shabbos-goy* all by ourselves.

I am not yet racist at this stage of my life. Though racism is in the molecules of the air I breathe and will eventually infiltrate my body, as yet I have no sense that whites are superior. I am much more aware of the difference between Jews and Gentiles than of the difference between whites and Coloureds.[9]

When I am around three or four, my cousin Ora from Israel comes to live with us. She is three years older than my 17-year-old sister Shulamit and teaches kindergarten in a Jewish school in the Southern Suburbs. Her father, Yosef, my father's elder brother in Israel, sends her to live with us to avoid the dangerous run-up to the 1948 Israeli War of Independence. Once, we were all Dereczynskis; now, we in South Africa are all Dermans, but Yosef and his family have taken the Hebrew surname Dror, meaning freedom.

Yosef lives in Tel Aviv and is a big shot in the Israeli Maritime League, the organization of the Israeli merchant fleet. He has a solid presence, bulkier and more reassuring than the skinnier brothers here in Cape Town. He is masculinely handsome, but his wife, Peshe, is short and fat, squashed and frog-like in my young eyes. Yosef may be a womaniser. I hear my mother once tell how Peshe says: "They can have what they can get, but I'm the real Mrs Dror." When she dies Yosef marries a Jewish woman who is French and beautiful.

Ora is a Sabra. She has her father's handsome looks but a sharp scary tongue. She makes Shulamit's life miserable by ridiculing her un-Israeli bourgeois practice of wearing lipstick and make-up. But Ora is good to me. I am only three but she vocally praises and admires my long eyelashes and blue eyes. In 1948, at the first-ev-

9 In those days there were many fewer Blacks than Coloureds in the Western Cape and in my environs.

er Yom Ha'Atzmaut Israeli Independence Day celebration in Cape Town, she lifts me high in the air – I can feel her hands under my armpits now – and places me on one of the floats for the parade at the Rosebank fairgrounds. And she cuts out and collects all the "Thought for the Day" items from the *Cape Times* and sticks them in an autograph book with beautiful pastel pages for my mother.

My mother hasn't seen her Israeli sisters and brother since the early 1930s in Brest and so we set off on a trip to Israel in December 1949 when I am four-and-a-half. My father is depressed around this time, perhaps because of business. *"Ich kan mehr nicht onge-hen,"* Ruth hears my father say to my mother late at night in their bedroom before we travel. *I can't carry on anymore.*

Ruth is the source of all my images from that time. She is my main educator and my main companion at home, dominant in my memory. She teaches me to read phonetically before I am ready for school, and to write. As she moves through high school, she practises for her exams by reciting or explaining to me what she needs to know: her high school history books, the plots of George Bernard Shaw plays, and English poetry. She teaches me the Christmas carols they learn in school. She takes her Brownie camera to Israel and photographs everything.

We embark for Johannesburg, where we stay a night or two with relatives of relatives. There is a photo of me on a swing. I fall and bloody my white shirt. From there we fly in a Douglas DC-4 Sky-master, puddle-hopping our way north through Africa with many stops. We are never above the weather, and never fly at night. It is bumpy and everyone has a bag to vomit into, and they do.

Our first stop is Nairobi, at an overnight hotel. My mother bathes me before bed while I stand on a stool in the white bathtub. I slip and scrape my back. When we refuel the next day, the air hostess shows me our dessert, a huge, freshly picked bunch of small tropical yellow bananas that are stored behind the last passenger seats at the back.

In Entebbe on Lake Victoria, Ruth buys a little carved tribal black-and-yellow wood statuette of a man. Later, she transforms it into a good luck charm that she takes in her pencil case to exams for years afterwards, and then bequeaths to me when she finishes university. She also keeps with it, for luck, too, a small piece of matzah, part of the Passover *Afikoman* that she replaces with a new piece each year. She teaches me to do the same: I, too, religiously take both statuette and each year's stolen Afikoman in my pencil case to exams, all through school and university, until I lose the statuette somewhere in New York soon after I arrive in 1966. I think it must have fallen outwards off the window sill of my room in International House.

En route to Khartoum, an enormously fat man on our plane has a heart attack after eating large quantities of pickled meat somewhere over equatorial Africa. When we land, very black men in shorts, blacker than I've ever seen, meet us on the tarmac in the intense heat and escort us into the shade of a shack while we refuel. They take the fat man away.

We touch down in Wadi Halfa too. Then, because of some mechanical problem, we are redirected to Cyprus, where people draw lots to get on the next plane to Tel Aviv. Somehow, someone offers us one of their seats to keep us all together. My relatives embrace us at Lydda airport. I recognise no one except Ora, who picks me up in her arms and says she wants to see if I still have those blue eyes.

In Israel it is the *famously cold winter* of 1949–50. We live with my aunt Naomi and her ginger-haired husband Chanina in Ramat Gan on Rechov Herzl in their small flat. We've never seen snow in South Africa, so Shulamit, now sixteen or seventeen, heads off to the heights of Jerusalem, hoping to see the snow that has been forecast. Instead, it snows right where we are, on the coast in Tel Aviv, and we all wear pyjamas underneath our clothes for warmth. Ruth has photos of us in front of the snowman we build, our pyjama bottoms and tops peeping out.

Food is scarce after both World War II and the War of Independence, and my aunt Yafa takes me to a coupon bureau where she pleads for the right to get me an extra banana.

People give me rooster-shaped red lollipops, which I now realise must have originated in Russia.

We eat corn on the cob that street vendors fish out of steaming barrels of hot water on dark street corners.

In nearby fruit orchards, Ruth, my cousin Shaul, and I steal a few grapefruit from a tree and run away. We peel them like oranges and are disappointed at their sourness.[10]

I get a toy tank with treads and a friction motor which I push back and forth on the sociable balcony that all Israeli apartments have.

I get an old-fashioned metal spark gun with flint inside that fires sparkling tracers when you pull the trigger.

10 Today no one can imagine how sour grapefruit used to be.

Vivid in my head are the blood-red eyeballs of my little cousin Rivka, two or three years younger than me and named after my mother's mother – her pram had been struck by a runaway truck whose brakes had failed. I like to push Rivka's pram around when they let me, and this is perhaps when I become fond of her, a life-long affection even though I see her rarely. She has the features and temperament of my mother's side of the family, a rarity.

One afternoon some friends of my parents take us for a sight-see-ing drive away from Ramat Gan and Tel Aviv. Somewhere along the way, I hear one of them point out a nearby jail.

"But why is there a jail here?" I ask from the back seat. "Isn't everyone Jewish?"

Chapter 4
Deaths, Girls, Songs

Wish me luck as you wave me goodbye, Cheerio here I go on my way • Seeking the love of women and girls • The thrilling power of romance

MORE DEATHS: CHICKENS, CATS, GENERAL SMUTS

We live at 320 Victoria Road until I am seven. The house has its own deep adventure hideouts. The best are navigated with my cousin Abner who lives nearby. There is a decrepit "chicken hok" at the back, a wire-fenced chicken coop where we sometimes hide in order to "smoke" drinking straws whose ends we set on fire. Sometimes my mother comes home with a slaughtered chicken – from the *sho-*

chet to whom she took one of our live ones or from the market where she bought a dead one? – that has to be repeatedly rotated over a flame to loosen and remove the quills.

Some afternoons Abner and I hide out in an old garage at the back of the garden and explore piled-high boxes of old magazines and books left there by the previous occupants. Once, in the gated and trellised orchard with fully grown but neglected fruit trees, we somehow manage to tie my sister Ruth to a tree with a rope until she cries, and we have to let her loose.

There are hordes of feral cats patrolling the garden, living in the garage, seemingly everywhere, and someone comes to kill them all. There is lots of blood. I'm taken away while it happens.

In 1950 the wireless plays frequent news bulletins about the declining health of ex-Prime Minister Jan Smuts during his terminal illness. He was the head of the United Party, the main opposition to the Nationalists. I have a little wooden toy soldier that I place carefully balanced on his narrow feet in a little wagon that I pull by a string around our house over floors and carpets. If my soldier falls over during my circuit around the house, Smuts will die. If not, he will live.

THE POWER OF WOMEN AND GIRLS

In kindergarten, when I am four or perhaps five, there is a young woman teacher who is affectionate to me. One day she suddenly begins to keep her distance. My sister Shulamit, years later, says that the young woman must have been reprimanded for showing favourites. It's an abandonment I don't remember much about, just its occurrence. However, one day I (surreptitiously?) take some plasticine home from the classroom. Do I know it's wrong? I think so. Is it related to the now unaffectionate teacher? I don't know. Nudged by my parents, I return the plasticine the next day at school.

In those days, teachers had no problem with cuddling children. Here is a photo of the kindergarten classes together on the steps of the school. Every lady teacher has her hands on a child, a display of affection *verboten* today. I am third from the right in the second row from the back.

I am five years old when I enter Sub A, the first year at real school. Ruth has taught me to read and write during the previous year, and after a few weeks, they move me up to Sub B, their name for Second Grade. The teachers are stricter now. I am at a desk at the back of the row. Miss Noah refuses to let me go to the toilet. Alfred giggles as the floor beneath my desk pools. At break, I walk solitarily around the enclosed playground with my face and pants to the wall. Arriving home, I run up the walkway to my mother, in tears.

One day a plump full-faced pretty new girl named Aida enters our class. Her family had emigrated to Israel and then returned to Cape Town. In the playground before school starts, while we mill around, I give her my new pencil sharpener, a small blue globe with a map of the earth on it. "Even though you gave it to me, I still don't like you," she says.

There are other insults. Miss Salomon, pale, stocky, red-haired and freckled, lives around the corner from our house on Victoria Road. She is my teacher in school and also a friend of my sister Shulamit, so she sometimes comes to our house after school. She arrives when my mother is putting forkfuls of lunch into my mouth, feeding me like a baby while I read a book – anything to get me to eat. Miss Salomon mocks me for being spoiled, right there in my parents' house. Later, when she teaches us to write letters to people in English class, she shames me publicly for signing my school letter to my sisters "Love, Emanuel." I should have written "Yours sincerely."

There is a small pretty dark girl I like who seems different from everyone else, though I don't know why. She is Sandra Naidoo, the five-year-old daughter of a South African Indian father and a white Jewish mother, both members of the South African Communist Party, which is banned in South Africa. Some all-Jewish, all-white parents of other children have complained about having a non-white but still Jewish child in the school, an arrangement now against government policy. Soon, she is gone.

THE POWER OF ROMANCE

At home my mother sings cheerful-sad WWII songs: *Wish me luck as you wave me goodbye, Cheerio here I go on my way. Give me a smile I can keep all the while in my heart while I'm away.* She likes the nonsensical *Chi-baba Chi-baba* by Peggy Lee. Ruth listens to the upbeat, carefree pre-rock American pop music that has swept the world. *If I knew you were coming I'd have baked a cake, Choo choo choo choo Choo'n gum,* and *Music Music Music* by Teresa Brewer. Ruth plays the piano well and practices hard. Her music teacher, severe Mrs Dober, feels free to rap her knuckles with a little bamboo stick. It's allowed. Ruth has classical records, including Tchaikovsky's Violin Concerto in D, Op. 35, which requires playing many successive extra-large 12-inch 78 rpm vinyl records, a few minutes on each side, in order to capture the whole interrupted concerto.

Those songs are merely catchy. Our maid, though, listens to Nat King Cole and sings his songs about romance. I learn to croon *They try to tell us we're too young, too young to really be in love,* which brings me welcome attention from adults. A few years later, our new maid throws her entire soul into *Unchained Melody.* I'm not sure how, but very early in life, I grasp from them something about love's power and danger.

Chapter 5
"For This I Didn't Come to South Africa"

Elegant in Slonim • Hardscrabble in Cape Town • Jealously in love • Her tombstone: Why did he do this immensely untraditional thing?

My father was born in 1902, three years earlier than my mother, in Slonim, Poland. Not only does he stick to his Hebrew name, but unlike anyone else I know, he stubbornly observes the Hebrew calendar as far as his birthday is concerned. So, every year, my sisters and I have to figure out the Gregorian date corresponding to the 2nd day of *Chol HaMoed, Sukkot*, which is somewhere around September/October.

Eliyahu Moshe Dereczynski, Born 1840 in Slonim, Died 1912
Menahem Mendel Dereczynski, Born 1866 in Slonim, Died 1912
Chaim Dereczynski, Born 1902 in Slonim, Died 1985

When my father was ten years old, in 1912, his father, Menahem, died suddenly while he was sitting Shiva for his father, Eliyahu, in

Slonim. My father never talks about it, though it must have made life hard. (Years later, when his five-year-old grandson asked him if it was true that people were buried in the ground when they died, my father thought we shouldn't confirm it for him.) My father's mother, Henye Leah, took over their dry goods business and single-handedly brought up six boys and one girl.

He married when he was 30. I don't know what he did in Poland for a living. He may have been a teacher; he may have worked in the dry goods store his mother ran. Perhaps both. He also says he studied some Talmud.[11] But in the photo below of him with friends in Slonim, they look sophisticated and European: beautiful dresses, elegant suits and ties. Astonishingly for me, he rests his hand on the leg of the young woman to his right. Once, he mentions to me how he used to get manicures, something pointless and unthinkable now that he works with his hands. He wears no wedding ring; he injured his finger in the garage once, and they had to cut through the ring to get it off.

Already married, he was the last of his brothers and sisters to make it out of Poland to Cape Town. When he got there, he changed his

11 In Chaim Grade's Yiddish short story *Laybe-Layzar's Courtyard*, a young man goes to study in the famous yeshiva in Slonim. My father loved Chaim Grade's poetry, and it made me feel good to notice, recently, that Chaim Grade and his wife Inna are buried in the cemetery affiliated with my synagogue.

name from Dereczynski to Derman, as those before him had done. He left my mother and my sister Shulamit behind in Poland for two years until he got settled.

On his arrival in Cape Town in 1934 his mother arranged for him to work in a butcher shop with his younger brother Ephraim in Retreat, a run-down dangerous shabby suburb, really just a bare main road surrounded on both sides by sand dunes on which poor Cape Coloured people live in scattered corrugated-iron shanties. "For this, I didn't come to South Africa," he told his mother in Yiddish after a few days, and proceeded to set up his own garage. My uncle Ephraim still lives out there near Retreat, in Jewish suburban beach-side Muizenberg, and continues to run the butcher shop. As a child, I often spend a few days in summer with Uncle Ephraim and Aunt Jeanette, and I play with my cousin Ronnie. Sometimes we visit the butcher shop, and Ronnie shows me the revolver his father keeps in the drawer under the serving counter. Coloured people who have no running water walk across the dunes to the shop to fill a bucket with water and then schlep it back to their shanty.

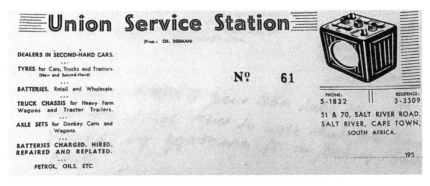

My father is more entrepreneurial than I will ever be. During WWII there was a shortage of car batteries in South Africa – they were all imported. After studying the manufacture of batteries and after much bureaucracy begging, he got permission to import the supplies to manufacture batteries himself and sell them to his customers. In a warehouse upstairs in the back of the garage, he and his assistant David learn to melt lead and cast it into thin lattice-like plates with a large surface area, which they then place inside imported black bakelite battery cases. They fill the case with dilute sulphuric acid, check the concentration with a hydrometer, and close the bakelite screw top. My mother works with him in the upstairs battery factory too, sometimes helping with acid preparation. "You have to pour acid into water when you dilute it, not water into acid," my father tells me when I begin to learn chemistry. "That way it's the water that splashes back at you rather than the acid." He continues making his own brand of batteries for years. The white cotton lab coat he wears over his clothes in the garage has brown acid-tinged burn holes. When my mother begins to have neurological troubles in the 1970s, the doctors first suspect it's the consequence of inhaling the fumes from the molten lead involved in battery-making. In fact, she has amyotrophic lateral sclerosis. In the late 1950s, my father tires of garage work and eventually reinvents himself as a well-to-do developer of commercial property.

He always encourages me to be an academic, to have a career that you can take anywhere in the world, because that's how it may have to be if you are Jewish. It's ironic that I end up in physics in the 1970s, a vocation that, conversely, requires me to go wherever there is a university job, and there aren't many. I think sometimes of Freud, who, in *Civilisation and Its Discontents*, wrote: "If there had been no railway to conquer distance, my child would never have left town and I should need no telephone to hear his voice."

My mother, even more so, nudges me toward academia rather than business. It's classier somehow. Business is how you make your living, but study – that's on a higher level. My father is dead by the time I have a successful career in business, and I suspect he would have been more proud of that than of my academic life.

My father is stubborn and can be difficult, but my sisters are furiously proud of him and his talents – we inherit from him what we have in that domain. He is very clever, knows maths, reads Yiddish literature, and writes Yiddish poems that get published in journals abroad, but he doesn't share them with us. He says he is an atheist. He says the invention of the Sabbath as a day of rest is the greatest innovation of the Jewish people. He says the three people that had the greatest influence on the 20th century were Marx, Freud, and

Einstein, all Jewish. Once when I am fifteen he amazes me and my classmates by intuitively solving our assigned high school algebra problem about filling a tank with water from the top that has a leak on one side a few inches above the bottom. My best friend Howie still periodically retells the story to this day.

Unlike my stoic mother, my father is prone to sentimentality. After the Israeli Suez Campaign of 1956, when young Israeli soldiers were killed in the Negev desert, tears come to his eyes whenever he hears Yaffa Yarkoni's Israeli song *B'Arvot HaNegev* about a fallen youth and his grieving mother. His Yiddish poems are about the lost loves of young boys and girls. He has a tendency to brood and suffers from separation anxiety, too. He becomes moody, low and agitated when my mother goes alone to Israel to visit her sisters and brother in the early 1960s and frequently cables and calls her to come back. Shulamit and I hear him pacing at night. He pressures her to return, and, sooner than she intended, she does. He depends on her. And perhaps he is jealous of my mother's wrong-side-of-the-tracks former Polish love, who may live in Israel now.

CONTRADICTIONS

At home we keep kosher. We have four sets of cutlery and crockery: one each for milk and meat, and another set of each specifically for Passover. My father is stricter than the rest of us. His name is his Hebrew name and his birthday is on the Jewish calendar. He won't drink coffee with milk after a meat meal, even though he's not a believer. Customs are very important to him. And yet ...

A year after my mother dies in 1979, my father composes the inscription for her tombstone. Later when I read it, I (and I alone) notice he has done something tremendously and almost incomprehensibly strange:

On Jewish tombstones it's customary to write the English name and surname of the deceased in the Latin alphabet and the Jewish patronymic name in the Hebrew alphabet. On his tombstone, six years after my mother's death, he is *Chaim Ben Menahem Mendel*, in Hebrew. My mother's correct patronymic is *Chaya Sara Bat Nahum Zvi*. But for her tombstone, my father arranged for her Jewish name to appear as simply "Sonia Derman," transliterated into Hebrew. No one notices this anomaly except me. Her patronymic is absent; only the "Derman" remains.

Why did he do this immensely untraditional thing? Was he aware of what he did? Why no reference to her father? Why identify her only as a Derman? Was he trying to claim her irrevocably for himself?

I notice it too late to find out.

Chapter 6
Charton, Woodburn Crescent, Oranjezicht, Cape Town, South Africa, The World, The Solar System, The Universe

When it's warmer the pine tree cones sporadically let loose individual pine nuts in their hard dark powdery shells.

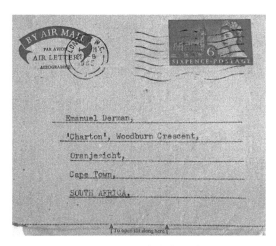

Salt River, where we live in my early childhood, is a poor neighbourhood which Jewish people are moving out of. Howie, my best friend at school, says that when he told his mother[12] about his new friend, she asked him where the friend lived. When he told her "Salt River," or perhaps "Woodstock," she asked him if he couldn't find a friend from a better place.

12 Born in South Africa, she was likely more attuned to the social status of new immigrants than the immigrant parents of most of the children in our school.

I have no knowledge yet about the stigma of the neighbourhood I live in, but I do know about the stigma of bankruptcy. There is one boy in my class whose father, I overhear from adult table talk, went bankrupt, and though I don't know what that means, I know that it's a shame and a disgrace. I see him in the playground at school and feel sorry for him.

I am seven years old when we move from poor Salt River to classier Oranjezicht, where we have bought a house. To accomplish this, my father went to an actual on-the-street auction where men congregate in front of a house at an appointed time and shout competitive bids to the rapid-talking auctioneer.[13] In Salt River we live on level ground not far from Table Bay. Now, in Oranjezicht, we are high above town and overlook it.

Our house is on Woodburn Crescent — such an elegant English street name! — running off long steep two-way Molteno Road which rises up against gravity from just above town until it peters out on the bare slopes of Table Mountain where baboons roam.

Woodburn Crescent, the wall of our house on the left, and my Fiat 1500 of 1963 parked in front.

13 Auctioneers and radio rugby sports announcers are admired for their capacity to keep up an uninterrupted stream of words, and I have friends who like to imitate them and aspire to become one or the other. Both those professions seem glamorous.

And our house has an actual name, Charton. It sounds like an English estate out of Agatha Christie: *The Mysterious Affair at Charton*. My mother says that it was much more prosaically named by the previous Jewish family that lived there, the Velkeses, so as to incorporate the name of the father, *Char*les, and his son, *Ton*y. They moved further upscale to Sea Point after we bought their house.

Charton is a double-storey home on a steep slope that has been terraced – the land slopes here since we are on the lower part of Table Mountain. The terraces rise from level to level, like rice-paddy terraces in Vietnam.

The house and its terraces are way above street level, contained by a white wall separating them from the street. On the lower terrace at the front of the house are several separate lawns; on either side of the house, flower gardens ascend on several higher terraces; finally, at the back of the house, the highest terrace has grape vines growing on trellises. Then, a fence marks off the end of our property, beyond which is wild tree-filled ground that has never been cleared for housing. We have a fig tree and tens of pine trees all around.

Charton. My bedroom is at the top in the centre, a once open porch that has been enclosed by windows.

To the left of the house is a garage with wooden doors. Its flat cement roof lies a few feet above the first terrace and its lawns. From that roof my friends and I can Batman-jump onto a nearby lawn while wearing towels tied around our necks.[14] My mother harvests our own grapes to make sweet kosher Passover wine that she ferments in a small barrel she keeps in the dark garage.

The house is large and very solid. Unlike many American houses, it's made of brick and concrete and nothing shakes when you bound up the stairs. The ground floor has a "breakfast room(!)," a dining room, a lounge (yes, that's what we call it), and a kitchen, with a long corridor connecting them. We eat all our meals in the cheery breakfast room and use the dining room only when visitors come for a more formal meal. For dessert we sometimes serve them strawberries from the garden. In the kitchen, on the wall high above the door, is an electrical board and bell, broken and never to be repaired but reminiscent of *Upstairs, Downstairs*. It shows which room has rung for the servants. On the first floor are three bedrooms but only a single bathroom for everyone. The bedrooms are allocated, one each to my parents, Shulamit, and Ruth. I get to sleep in a long glassed-in upstairs porch that faces the street and has light coming in on three sides.

Looking down the mountainside from the house I see Table Bay, looking up, the mountain and its slopes. The higher parts of Oranjezicht are half unbuilt, dense with wild trees. Behind the back border of our garden are acres of saplings that fill up most of the block between Woodburn Crescent and the similarly named Crescent above. You can vanish completely as you part the bushes and trees to play in the jungle. You can find branches to make into bows and arrows, and trees to tie people to.[15]

The cement backyard the kitchen door opens onto has a storage room at one end that I use as a darkroom when I'm older. At the other end is the small maid's room for Rosie, our new Coloured maid. In all the years I subsequently lived there, I never entered her room.[16]

---

14 I always want to be Batman. He has a better sense of humour than Superman.

15 Yes, we do that sometimes to one particular friend when we capture him in a cowboy adventure.

16 Similarly, Doris Lessing in her autobiography remarks that she has never seen

But, every day, I see Rosie in our house; in the evenings, I hear her darker boyfriend Walter visiting her; in the block of flats opposite, I see the buzzing community of maids living in their ground-floor rooms. And so I internalise the connection between roles and races. It's observing them in a community of their own that crystallises the perception of differences.

Our neighbours on Woodburn Crescent and in Oranjezicht are mostly immigrant Jewish families. I have no clue that there are different types of Jews – German and East European. Much, much later, when I return to Cape Town after living in New York, I visit my high school and tell our principal I am getting married. "Not to a Polish Jew, I hope," he says, (perhaps) jokingly. I have never heard any remark about Polish Jews before.[17]

I have a more fluid existence in our new house. In Salt River, I never had a street or outdoor life. Here there are enough lawns in our garden to improvise a rope between a pine tree and a hedge and then practise high jump. One lawn is long enough to bowl cricket balls. There are secret places where you can hide and not be seen from the house. After the rain, the drops of water dripping off the thick leaves of cactus-y plants smell richly pure, and my cousin Leopold and I convince each other it's an anaesthetic we can use to put adults to sleep. When it's warmer, the pine trees all around the house let loose, from their hand-grenade cones on high, bursts of individual pine nuts in their hard dark powdery shells. You can hear them fall. Friends come over to search for the dennepits on the grass lawns or on the gravel paths between, collect them, crack them open on our cement garage roof with a small stone, and eat the pignola inside. They're a free luxury. Some of us first collect a whole bunch, thirty or forty, then take them to the top of the garage, crack them one by one without giving in to temptation, and

the inside of their servant's room in 1940s Southern Rhodesia.

17 I understood only later, having left Cape Town, that our neighbours were mostly Lithuanian Jews, with a few German Jews interspersed and a smattering of Gentiles.

then finally stuff a whole handful of the kernels into the mouth. Others, myself among them, crack them as we find them, eating one after the other.

The house is large enough to play games in. Howie and I invent a miniature golf in which you have to stroke the ball down the corridor and through various rooms using an old walking stick. The fewest strokes count the most. In the living room, we play "balloon soccer," with each goal being a wall at the end of the room. You and your opponent face each other and then take turns punching the balloon towards the wall opposite you. To add tactical complexity and interest, we rule that you can get a second successive punch if your first punch manages to make the balloon hit the floor ahead of you before your opponent can reach it and punch back.

My mother drives my father to the garage in Salt River early every morning. Sometimes she drives me to school and sometimes I get a ride with Clark and Leopold in a white Studebaker of Uncle Simcha's, who lives five minutes away on Glen Crescent. Often, in the winter rain, my mother's big Chevrolet has trouble starting in the morning, and she devises a way to coax it by placing a hot water bottle or two under a blanket on top of the spark plugs for ten minutes. It usually works. If it doesn't, she gets someone to push her to Molteno Road, and then, letting the car run downhill with the clutch in, she starts it without battery power by letting the clutch out so the gears engage and turn the pistons, which then start firing. The ride will charge the battery.

There is no winter heating in Cape Town houses, and my father and I, separately, like to sit and read in our Chevrolet greenhouse parked on the street on weekend winter afternoons, deliciously warm. Failing that, we read in bed with a hot water bottle under the blankets, even in the daytime.

Chapter 7
~~Joseph~~ Chaim and His Brothers

*"I am a Polish Jew, and I doubt if there is any community that
has more thieves in it than the Polish one."*

The Dereczynskis were plopped down on foreign soil on the southern tip of Africa. They came here in waves, the first cousins of ours
as early as the turn of the 19th century, the subsequent ones following their trail. They took ocean liners from Europe to London and
then London to Cape Town. The last to arrive, my father Chaim,
came in 1933. By then, three of his brothers and a sister were settled here, and his mother too.

Though they came in the nick of time, they were *not* fleeing Hit-
ler and the Germans; it was too early for that. They were merely
abandoning Poland. My father once reminisced about how, when
the Germans captured Slonim from the Russians in 1915, people in
the town rejoiced.

Without money or professions, immigrant family members had
to make a living. The foreign-born wives worked. The men, and the
women too, did hardscrabble things, hustled to start businesses,
and were poorer and less elegant than they had been back home.
They did what they had to and most of them prospered, but the
struggle coarsened them. They helped each other but they also
competed. In mutual help and in mutual competition, blood was
thicker than water.

The extended family lies in concentric circles around my parents, sisters, and me. I know, without a second thought and without
it ever having been spelled out, who is in which circle, who is like us
and who is different.

In the closest circle are my father's three local brothers, Lezer, Ephraim, and Simcha, and his sister Esther.

For now, we are all thick as thieves. We live in and out of each other's houses. We have huge joint Passover seders at which my sister Ruth dresses up as Elijah the prophet, donning a white cotton wool beard and handing out presents to the eleven cousins when the front door is opened and everyone sings *Eliyahu HaNavi* in anticipation of the prophet's Santa-Claus-like visit.

The uncles and aunts in this circle are irredeemably foreign, born in Poland, and speak heavily accented English.

The second circle contains numerous second and third cousins. Some of them have the same names as our closer relatives: one second cousin is also named Ephraim, and another, Sam, has a wife named Jeanette. To avoid confusing them in conversation, they get Yiddish monikers. We all refer to my father's brother Ephraim as *Unsere Ephraim* (Our Ephraim, in Yiddish) to distinguish him, a brother, from the shorter second cousin *Ephraim der Kleiner* (Ephraim the Small One). Similarly, Ephraim's Jeanette is called *Unsere Jeanette* to distinguish her from the other cousin's wife, whom everyone calls *Jeanette Semmes* (Jeanette belonging to Sam, her husband). In English, she is always referred to as "JeanetteSams," in one word.

For the second circle as well as the first, my mother is a listener and helps with their problems. My sister Shulamit, when she later becomes a social worker, is the go-to for any difficulties that need professional help.

Beyond are the more distant relatives, the comfortably assimilated ones whose parents immigrated thirty years or more earlier than my parents did. We see them only at weddings, Bar Mitzvahs, and funerals. They have otherworldly skills and desires that go beyond subsistence: they have no accent, they can speak Afrikaans, they go fishing, they have speedboats. They have leisure time and hobbies outside of work. They might even play golf. They are halfway to being *goyim,* classier than we are but less trustworthy, less family-centred.[18] We aren't completely comfortable with them. They know the ropes.

CHAIM AND SIMCHA

Uncle Simcha, the youngest of my father's brothers, is charismatic, urbane, charming, good-humoured. He's the most popular uncle. While my father looks wan and uncomfortable in family photos, Simcha rests at ease in his chair, smiling. He is sociable and smooth: he gets on Jewish school committees, has people over to play rummy at his and Aunt Lizzie's house.

We spend the most time with him and Lizzie and their two boys: Clark, three years older than I am, and Leopold, my age. ("Clark" is inspired by Clark Gable, and I have no idea where the Germanic "Leopold" comes from.)

My sisters and I feel Simcha's charm and smoothness too. But there is an iron hand beneath his velvet touch, and it crunches relatives who get on his wrong side.

My father is Esau, Simcha is Jacob.

Simcha married a first cousin once removed. There is blood between them. Lizzie is a genuine South African, born in a nondescript dorp on the edge of the Karoo north of Cape Town. She is the eldest daughter of a first cousin of my father's who came from Slonim many years earlier. She is very very round and very very fat and exceedingly jolly, always eating diabetic gumdrops though she is not diabetic. Periodically, she goes on diets that involve consuming vast amounts of papaya to lose weight, and her skin turns yellow.

The other brothers and their wives whisper about Simcha's business dealings. If you can believe them – although no one will talk about it explicitly – he has somehow ruined various relatives' businesses, taken away their customers, and revelled with Lizzie in

18 My mother has a favourite story about the child of one of them, eight-year-old Richard. He was ill in bed with a high fever and his South-African-born mother sat beside him, soothing him and putting Eau de Cologne on his brow. "Richard my dear, will you look after me one day too, when I'm old and sick?" she asked him. "Why do you always pick on me, why don't you sometimes pick on Leon and Jonathan?" he replied with irritation, referring to his two older brothers.

their misfortunes. The ruined relatives refuse to visit him, but he courts their children and wives with hospitality. The nephews and nieces visit him while their fathers won't go to his house.

But my father likes Simcha and helps him in various ventures. They collaborate, they sound each other out on business ideas. And he is our favourite too. When Ruth turns twenty-one in 1957, it is Uncle Simcha and Aunt Lizzie who come with our family to have dinner at the Schweizerhof in Cape Town, where, to everyone's wonder, the restaurant serves us melba toast, the latest delicacy.

Lizzie is jolly but has OCD tendencies. She undergoes periods of obsessive worry and Simcha sends her to my mother to help calm her down. My mother listens to her repetitive anxieties. Once, after her young nieces visit from Israel for a few weeks, she is obsessed with the fear that she had damaged their health by what she had fed them. The chicken she had prepared for them had had a few spots of blood inside its body before she cooked it. Perhaps it wasn't completely kosher? The milk they drank had been in the refrigerator too long. Could it have stunted their growth? Simcha begs my mother to help ease her agitation. My mother listens ceaselessly to Lizzie, trying to talk sense into her.

We are in the habit of spending Friday nights after dinner at Simcha and Lizzie's, the women talking, the men playing rummy for money, the kids playing in the bedroom. My father, less sociable, loves to be part of the card-playing circle that Simcha has invited for an evening. Sometimes I sleep over at their house, Clark and Leopold and I in two beds pushed next to each other. One morning I awake to find Leopold licking my face.

Clark and Leopold are wild, much wilder than any other cousins. They fight each other, can be subdued only by Lizzie's threat that their father will see to them when he comes home.

They have many more material goods than I have:

- Fair Isle sweaters imported from England;
- an electric train;

- a table-tennis table that fills up a spare bedroom;
- a Bayko set for building toy houses;
- a toy cricket game you play on a green table-top mat on which the bowler rolls the ball down an inclined V-shaped metal flange, the batter is a little pendulum controlled by pulling and releasing a string, and the fielders are stationary plastic men with pockets in their feet to hold the ball if it hits them. I really like that cricket game.

When space travel is in the offing, they get 1950s toy space suits with plastic helmets.

Are they much richer than we are? It never occurs to me to ask.

My mother won't pay to buy me Fair Isle sweaters like those they have. She knits her own version for me and it's just as good. She sews her own dresses that people admire. She has a Singer sewing machine, with a treadle, that she can expertly use. She knows how to fix its insides when the spools of cotton thread tangle. She embroiders beautiful tablecloths with cross-stitching. She crochets. She sews me a pair of summer shorts from cotton when I am eight, which are both too tight and too loose. Once I decide to wear them without underpants and my testicle protrudes through one leg of the shorts. That is her only failure.

My cousin Clark is good at business-like things from early on. On Saturday mornings Uncle Simcha drives Clark and Leopold down to the Colosseum bioscope to see films, and sometimes I go with them. There is a supporting program of shorts with Jungle Jim and Tarzan and Dan Dare and maybe Gene Autrey or Roy Rogers. Before the program starts, and at intermission after the supporting program, boys wander up and down the aisles to trade comic books they've read for comic books they haven't. Clark arrives with an armful, a stack of maybe twenty or thirty, and walks up and down like a carnival barker, offering what he has and asking for what he wants. He also collects "householders," perforated sheets of assorted coloured adverts, much like sheets of postage stamps, that distributors put in your mailbox. We trade individual householders with each other to try to collect an entire matching set about some range of products. Clark has a natural gift for this.

Clark is proud of his good voice, is in the synagogue choir, loves the film *The Great Caruso*, imitates Mario Lanza. He wants to be voted the best Bar Mitzvah of the year. He has a good sense of humour, is confident, has his own genuine charm. He is a bit round and pudgy, but physically strong, and sometimes has fierce fights with another ferociously bad-tempered neighbourhood boy in which they wrestle each other to the ground in the middle of the road and continue slamming each other's heads on the tarmac.

Leopold, three years younger, is strong but without his brother's lighter touch. His mother's OCD has filtered through. At age eight or nine, he has a mild bout of meningitis and is in the contagious ward of City Hospital. When I play with him afterwards back home in his room, he spends a lot of time rearranging things into the right locations on the table.

Both my cousins love business and its competitiveness.[19] My mother hears Lizzie bragging one day about how Leopold looks forward to cheating people when he grows up.

Twenty years later, Uncle Simcha and his sons cheat my father too. It costs my father dearly in spirit, and he fights them to the bitter end. Their family and ours break apart.[20]

My sisters continue the battle after he dies. Perhaps my father asked for it by having succumbed to Simcha's charm and to his own need for an associate, fully knowing Simcha's character and his previous misdeeds.

Blood will have blood. Twenty years more and Clark and Leopold battle each other over money and business. They never speak to each other again. In his sixties, in the USA, Leopold commits suicide.

---

19 My sisters and I are non-business people who have little interest in the details of our father's business. They study social work and psychology while I go into physics. We live off my father's business, yes, but somehow my mother has instilled in us the notion that we shouldn't pay attention to business and money. She has made us *luftmenschen* – at least until we get a lot older and realise what his money has made possible. Perhaps we are trying to have our cake and eat it, too? Maybe we fancy ourselves as better off than people who are more cultured and more cultured than people who are better off.

20 On being told that many Moroccan Jews were thieves, David Ben-Gurion said: "I am a Polish Jew, and I doubt if there is any community that has more thieves in it than the Polish one."

Chapter 8
In the Hood

*Cricketers, Servants, Afrikaners, Prost People, Lounging Ladies,
Liberace, Air Guns, The Immorality Act, Epileptics, Orphans,
and...Transcendence*

In Oranjezicht I have street friends and a street life, separate from
my parents and separate from school friends. There are boys and
girls everywhere in the houses and flats around us, boys on my
block, girls on many of the adjacent ones. And there are fascinating
people everywhere.

THE ASSIMILATED CRICKETER

Nearby, on the corner of Woodburn Crescent and Molteno Road,
lives Mr Abramowitz and his son Jack. I never see a Mrs Abramowitz. Mr Abramowitz is a really good cricketer and trains Jack in a
cricket net that he sets up on a full-length pitch spanning their two
long narrow lawns, divided by a concrete walkway in the middle.
He fast-bowls at his son, and very occasionally they let me have a
chance to hit a ball or two from Jack.

They're Jewish, but somehow, they don't seem Jewish – they're
too sporty and have no accent. They must have come here a long
time ago.

THE SCULPTOR

Opposite our house is a block of four flats. In one of them, on the
lower left facing the street, live the Josephsons, whose grown children are no longer at home. Mrs Josephson is a sculptor and gets
me to sit for hours at a time while she shapes a copy of me in grey
modelling clay. Between sessions she keeps the bust under a wet

cloth and inside a plastic bag to make sure it doesn't dry out. I get very impatient while sitting and often look at my watch. She decides that I am a very punctual, well-brought-up boy who is considerate about not keeping my parents waiting, but I am just eager to get out. Eventually, she finishes the head, casts it in plaster and exhibits it in a show where it garners praise in the local paper.

She gives me a hunk of modelling clay and an armature, and my mother buys me some wooden modelling tools, and I try to copy the head of me since no one else will sit for me.

LITTLE CHILDREN

In another flat are the Maisels, who have a cute two-year-old daughter I like to take photos of. Later, I colourise them with pigments and Q-tips the way people did when colour photos were much more expensive than black and white. Sometimes she cries and I like it because I can comfort her.

THE MAIDS OF THE FLATS

Every flat in the block has a Coloured maid and comes with a single maid's room on the ground floor at the back of the block where the maids live. A maid's work is never done: they make breakfast, make lunch, make dinner, can be called back late at night to clean up after a dinner with guests. Only in the backyard are they out from under anyone's thumb. There, we see and hear the maids' lively social lives with each other and their boyfriends after work at night. They keep their doors open and shout out to each other. They treat us kids like equals, exposing us to activities our parents would never talk about. Sometimes they tell us too much too soon. One of them points us to the discarded used condoms lying in the overgrown grass field at the side of the flats.

THE AFRIKANER SOCCER-BALL CONFISCATOR

In the house next to us are the childless Wilkens, Afrikaners and Afrikaans-speaking, almost the only non-Jewish people on the street. Their dog is called Pootsie, and it is small and yapping. Mr Wilken is a manager at the Volkskas, the big Afrikaner bank, and we all know they are Nationalists and pro-apartheid. The front of their house has no lawn but only a steep sloping rockery, separated from the street by a wire fence. They tend the rockery protectively. When we play soccer in the street, the leather ball sometimes goes over their fence and into their rockery, and Mrs Wilken refuses to let us retrieve it. These are our only interactions with her. We are wary of them, and I will have trouble with them later (see Chapter 18).

 THE THREE L'S

Down the road where the Crescent curves live the boys we call The Three L's: Leon, Leonard, and Leslie. They aren't friends of mine but denizens of the neighbourhood – my age, tougher, definitely not intellectual (if you can use that word for ten-year-olds). Years later, when I'm in New York, I come across an article in *The Economist* where someone is bragging about having worked with Leslie. He has become a famous director and cinematographer of commercials. "C'est la vie," say the old folks, it goes to show you never can tell.

LOUNGING LADIES

Where the Crescent curves, live the Felkowitzes. Mr Felkowitz is Lithuanian-born, surly and unpleasant, a businessman with a heavy accent. His wife is South African, doesn't work, and seems to lie palely and seductively around the house most days in elegant pyjamas near the picture window in their garden. One can't imagine them together. Their son, several years younger than me, can do mental arithmetic in his head but cannot explain how. If you give him a date in any year, he can tell you what day of the week it was. His mother worries about him. Sometimes, she asks me to involve him in more boyish activities, but he isn't interested.

PROST PEOPLE

On the Crescent below live the Silverbergs, born in South Africa, barely high-school educated, and snobbishly double-damned by my parents for not knowing much about Jewish culture either. Mr Silverberg is a flashy dresser and has a clothing store in District Six in the centre of the city, an area soon to be razed by the Nationalist government so that white people can occupy it. He speaks Afrikaans fluently. On occasion he beats his kids with a belt when they misbehave, chasing them around their bedroom until he catches them. When he curses it's in four-letter English words rather than obscure Polish or Yiddish ones. Mrs Silverberg is blowsy and skinny at the same time. She has long fingernails, each one painted in scarlet and silver, with the image of a tiny black spade or club straddling the diagonal where the colours meet. I play with their kids but I can tell my parents think the Silverbergs are *prost*. Or perhaps I no longer need their view. I'm old enough to get it myself.

LIBERACE FANS

Two houses over from ours live the Daniels. Their younger son Gerald, two years my junior, is another friend. He has a guitar and a Davy Crockett hat and a dazzling white smile and tells everyone that he looks like Liberace, who recently visited Cape Town. And it's true, he does. Gerald's parents, unlike most of the East European Jews that are my parents' friends, are German Jews with German accents, and they make him brush his teeth carefully. They are advanced enough to make sure he gets braces, an indulgence that never enters my parents' minds.

His brother is studying medicine, and Gerald periodically likes to recite the long Latin anatomical phrase that his brother has taught him: *levator labii superioris alaeque nasi.*[21]

FALLING EPILEPTICS

Opposite the Daniels lives an old couple, the Epsteins. They have a loquat tree that blossoms and bears fruit in the spring. You cannot buy loquats in any shop or market; they grow only in people's gardens. But they are delicious, and sometimes we break into the Epsteins' garden – there's just a low wall separating it from the street – and pick some. Old Mrs Epstein is epileptic, and sometimes, walking home from the bus stop ten minutes away, suddenly drops to the ground with a seizure we observe from our window.

BIRD KILLERS

There are older kids on our street, too. The Berlin family – father, mother, two teenage boys – live on the farther arm of Woodburn Crescent. Their two boys, probably six or seven years older than me, have *a pellet gun*! I know my parents will never buy me

---

21 He must have recited it often because I remember it clearly as a sort of poem which I'd never seen written down until I Googled it today.

one; I don't even ask for one. But I have used theirs. You bend back the steel barrel from the shoulder stock to open it; you insert a single rifled lead pellet, hollow at the back, into the cylindrical barrel; you reclose the barrel against the stock, which somehow compresses the air inside; you look through the sights and aim; then you pull the trigger.

The Berlin boys roam the little jungle behind our house and shoot small birds perched on branches who then plummet to the ground soundlessly. The boys leave them there. What is the point of killing something you didn't need to kill? Yet I am envious. Sometimes they let me take a shot myself, in their backyard where they have set up a rifle range with targets. I fire at a glass bottle. It's thrilling to pull the trigger and see the bottle turn opaque with internal cracks.

I will never get a pellet gun so I make myself a catapult, a Y-shaped tree branch with a piece of inner-tube rubber tied to each arm and a bit of leather to hold the stone. For ammunition, I know what to do. The back covers of the American comics we buy – Batman, Superman, Nancy and Sluggo, Little Audrey, Little Lulu – are plastered with ads for Daisy BB guns. I go to town on the bus to Jack Lemkus Sports and buy airgun pellets and caviar-like BB copper balls.

I shoot with my catapult outdoors at all kinds of things: bottles, cans, shoe boxes. I shoot even in my bedroom. I situate a bulls-eye target pasted onto a cardboard shoebox at one end of the room and shoot from the other end. Occasionally I take aim from our lawn above street level at a sparrow or pigeon in the trees or high up on the telephone wires that run along the road. Once, to my half horror, my metal pellet successfully hits the centre of the belly of a sparrow on the wire. It does not drop to the ground but flies away. What will become of it?

IMMORALITY ACT VIOLATORS

On Sunday mornings my father brings me the comic section of the *Cape Times* in bed so I can read the adventures of Prince Valiant or Brick Bradford and his Time Top. One morning on the front page of the main section is a story about Mr Berlin, the father of the two boys, a grey-haired rotund man. A lawyer in his forties, he was found on the floor of his town office with a young Black woman, a consummation that is illegal under the 1957 *Immorality Act*, the Nationalist government law that forbids intercourse between whites and non-whites. His doctor testifies that he had prescribed pills for Mr Berlin's heart condition. Was the Black woman also doing it because of the side effects of a medicine she had been given? I don't recall what sentence, if any, either of them received.

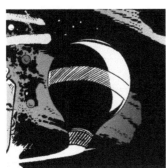 

THE ORPHANAGE

The Cape Jewish Orphanage is one street over from me, across Molteno Road on Garfield. The boys and girls there go to the same Jewish school I attend but they live in the orphanage. Some of them are genuine orphans, others are from "broken homes," and increasing numbers are not orphans at all, just Sephardic Jews who have come as refugees from the Belgian Congo where Belgian rule is now disintegrating.

The orphanage kids refer to themselves as being in "chook," a kind of criminal slang for prison. That seems not inaccurate. It never occurs to us for one moment to think about what it's like to live without parents to appeal to, without anyone to provide affectionate comfort or encouragement or help with homework. Perforce, the chook kids know how to negotiate with the world and experience its wounds alone. They must learn to self-comfort.[22]

22 A skill I find hard to acquire throughout my life. It took me years before I realised it was a skill at all, and that it was one that some people actually possessed.

No one I know really has *friends* from the orphanage. The orphanage kids seem to be friends mostly with each other. But the orphanage grounds are somehow open to everyone. *Habonim*[23], our Jewish youth group, meets in their hall and plays soccer on their virtually grass-bare field. After school, during marbles season, the orphanage kids run a marbles casino on their playground. They set up shies, little pyramids of stacked marbles at which you throw your own single marble from behind a distant line in the sand. If you hit the pyramid, you get all the marbles in it; if you miss, the shie proprietor keeps your marble. You might throw from ten feet at a pyramid of four – a triangle of three marbles at the base and one on top. A pyramid of ten – six marbles in a triangle at the base, then three, then one – requires that you stand much farther back to throw. Being the proprietor of a shie of ten is dangerous – one hit and you lose everything. Many of us go over there to play. Some of the chook boys manage to earn bags of marbles without parents like ours to provide them. One day I witness an orphanage boy build a giant multi-layered pyramidal shie with many marbles which you have to shoot at from very very far away. Someone strikes it successfully within a throw or two and takes them all. The boy bursts into sobs and runs away.

The orphanage grounds are a free-for-all with no adult supervision. One very short very tough red-haired boy in my class, a non-orphanage boy, likes to go there to display his penis to the orphanage girls.

SATURDAY NIGHTS

On Saturday nights when my parents go to bioscope, I get settled in bed in our new house before they leave. Rosie spends the evening in

23 See also Chapter 23.

her room outside and I am alone upstairs in the big double-storey listening to Springbok Radio, and I don't like it. I don't feel safe. Rosie has a boyfriend, Walter, who works at the orphanage a block away, and he comes to her room at night. She lets him through the gated back door to the backyard. I don't think I've ever seen Walter in the daytime. He is often drunk, and sometimes beats her or threatens to. From my room I can hear the scary shouting and fighting outside. One Saturday night at 11 p.m. she comes running into the house and locks the kitchen door. She boils a kettle full of hot water and pours it out of an upstairs window down onto Walter, who is standing by the kitchen door. A couple of nights later, when Walter comes by and drunkenly roams the garden trying to get to Rosie's room, my father cleverly goes to the window that faces the garden and shouts: *"Stand still, or I'll shoot!"* That does it.

THE PIPER AT THE GATES OF DAWN

On my tenth birthday Rosie wakes me up and tells me there's a girl to see me. She's grinning. I go downstairs and there in the hall by the front door is a new bicycle, with 26-inch wheels. It's a Hercules, made in England. Though many of my friends believe a Rudge is better, I'm happy with a Hercules. And it's three-speed.

I don't know how to ride a bike and don't know anyone who will teach me. My father isn't the kind of father who will put me on the bike, run behind me while pushing it, and then launch me into a mysterious moving equilibrium. And I'm not the kind of person to just get on and pedal fast and hope not to fall. There is, though, a 50- or 60-yard downward slope to the middle of Woodburn Crescent, and so I teach myself. I sit on the bike at the top of the slope, put my left foot on the sidewalk, my right foot on the pedal, and then scoot down the slope, using my left foot to support me when I tilt. Soon I am scooting longer distances, and from then on it's easy to add pedalling.

I get a mileometer on the front wheel and ride up and down the more or less flat connected stretch of Woodburn Crescent and Garfield Road, past the orphanage, over and over again. I add a playing card with a clothes peg to the front forks so that it will hit the spokes and make an engine sound. One day I do seventeen miles back and forth. I don't go far out of my immediate neighbourhood, nor does anyone else with a bike. To bike up Molteno Road to another level's Crescent is too difficult: the slope of the mountainside, with Molteno going straight up and the Crescents running like horizontal terraces, is so steep that to bike up to another terrace with only three gears means you have to get off and push. None of us use our bikes for transport. Only for fun.

On clear still-cool summer mornings I wake spontaneously at 7 am, carry my bike down the steps from our house to the street while everyone is still in bed, and start riding back and forth along Woodburn and Garfield. There is an older girl called Brenda who lives in a house on Garfield and I ring my bell loudly whenever I pass her house so that she will come to her window and talk. I have no idea that this ringing is too loud too early for her parents, who soon complain to mine.

At that time of the morning, riding my bike alone, the world is new and wonderful, beyond any experience I've had before. Something miraculous might happen.

Chapter 9
The Isle of Capri

Now that I've been given a bite of the apple, it's too late. Sex is everywhere.

After my four-year-old girl-kissing, I enter a latent period that lasts many years, my libido diverted into intellectual and sporting activities. I do like girls, but all I want is for them to like me back, *a lot. Dayenu.* Then, at the age of ten, some older boys inform me about the facts of life.

It happens in Montagu, a small town in a wine-making fruit-growing district about ninety miles inland from Cape Town. We go there regularly in wintry July for a week or two of holiday. To reach there my mother has to negotiate the steep and very narrow Bains Kloof Pass where mountains fall away precipitously from the open edge of the road. Montagu's main attraction is the local hot spring, which we believe is radioactive. Uncle Simcha and Aunty Lizzie and Clark and Leopold usually go there at the same time we do.

We stay a few miles outside the centre of Montagu proper, at the edge of a forest, in The Baths Hotel. The Baths is not classy at all. Wealthier families stay in the centre of Montagu itself, at The Avalon, a name that conjures up luxury and expense. At The Baths our bedroom is one of many in a long narrow two-storey building one room wide, covered with only a tin roof. It's not fancy. There is but one bathroom and one toilet at the end of each level, to be shared by all. If you want to urinate before you go to sleep, you have to walk down the open-air corridor along the rooms to the common W.C. and common bathroom at the end. In the middle of the night, if you don't want to make that trip in your pyjamas, you can take out from beneath your bed the heavy white enamelled chamber pot. The maid who cleans and tidies the room each morning empties it somewhere while we are out.

The main attraction of The Baths *is* the baths, the radioactive bubbling hot spring that fills up the swimming pool. The pool is wondrous, fifteen yards long, three sides man-made, the fourth a towering inward-slanting wall of rock from which emanates the hot spring. The cold air steams over the hot water; our breaths look like clouds. We stay in the water for hours. At age ten I learned from the teenage boys how to swim a full length underwater, sometimes managing a turn and going halfway back. At intervals, the Jewish ladies go into the pool to sit at the locus where the radioactive water enters. They let it pour over their arthritic shoulders and necks and sigh with Yiddish pleasure: *A Mechaye* (A joy, a reviver).

There is a long deep *kloof* (Afrikaans, a ravine) that separates The Baths from the centre of tiny Montagu. Packs of wild baboons roam there and sometimes come to scavenge on the hotel grounds, emptying trash cans and even entering rooms through open windows. An older boy I meet goes out to shoot at them with his pellet gun on the hills above the kloof. Our parents' and their friends' late morning routine is to take a several-mile constitutional from our hotel to Montagu centre through the kloof. At The Avalon, they eat scones with butter, jam, and whipped cream and pick up a Cape Town newspaper a day or two late. We kids stick to the grounds of The Baths, furiously socialising.

Every morning we get up early for breakfast with our families. It's cold in inland Montagu, unlike Cape Town, which is warmed by the sea. Your footprints leave clear traces on the frost-covered lawn in the early morning, and your fingers hurt and go red, but then by late morning, it warms up.

The menu at The Baths is classic South African British Colonial: boiled haddock for breakfast is one of the specialities, plus smoked kippers, stewed fruit, and various kinds of pudding. On our last day there, my cousin Clark forces himself to eat every dish on the menu the entire day in a kind of ritual annual challenge he has imposed on himself. During meals, while the men drink at most a beer and the women a beer shandy (beer with lemonade), we kids are allowed to order a ginger shandy, ginger beer with lemonade, the intense ginger beer providing a simulacrum of the perception of alcohol. The Black server who brings drinks to the table is formally called the Bar Steward. Clark likes to hail him by calling "Barsteward" loudly, eliding the words to make it sound like "bastard," good-humouredly from his point of view.

The Baths has its own flock of chickens kept in a fenced enclosure on the grounds. One day a week, we watch the cook's assistant go out to slaughter the chickens, chasing them around while they squawk and run. When he catches one, he simply chops its head off with an axe on a wooden plank. We watch hypnotically as the headless body flaps and jumps around. We decline chicken and chicken soup at lunch for a day or two, until the vision fades.

In the afternoons we play deck quoits with each other on a concrete strip, as though on board a ship. Our parents play garden bowls, which we sometimes try too, requesting the bowls from the front desk. You try to take advantage of the bias in the big black ball when you roll it on the flat grass and make it turn in. If we're not outside gossiping or flirting or playing, we are in the games room where there is an old piano and a table tennis table. My cousin Leopold, having a table at home, has always beaten me at table tennis. But now Ronnie Shell, whose parents have a dairy near where we used to live in Salt River, gives me a tutorial. A few years older than me, he is a crowned champion at junior table tennis in the Cape Province, and he teaches me to backhand-chop and forward-slice the ball to give it spin. The sliced ball bounces differently when it hits the table and veers off in unexpected directions. I play Leopold once and beat him by always chopping and slicing rather than slamming, while Ronnie encourages me from the sidelines.

I like to hang out with the older kids. One of them is a girl who is also on vacation in Montagu the year I turn ten. She is twelve or thirteen, older, vivacious. Her name is Rosa Ladny, from Sea Point in Cape Town. I've never known a girl with such a euphonious name – Rosa – before. She tosses her head and hair scornfully when she replies to boys' questions. Her mother is solidly built and has an acned face; her father is nondescript. The Ladnys are younger than my parents and walk together in an affectionate, almost sexy way that makes me think. Rosa's brother, a bit younger than me, is called Ivan. My mother remarks disparagingly on the name Ivan: it's a Russian peasant name, and why did they give a Jewish boy a Russian peasant name? But I am attracted to Rosa with the flashing eyes and dark looks. Clark, who can be funny, walks around pronouncing her name exaggeratedly as Roz-Uh-Lahd-Nee as though he were speaking what he imagines is Xhosa. He is not in her power as I am. I follow her around sometimes and try to get her attention. My father, who babies and embarrasses me with his accent, repeatedly brings me fruit to eat while I am outdoors with the other boys and girls. "My father doesn't run after *me* to bring *me* an apple in the middle of the day!" says Rosa scornfully. Ask not for whom the bell tolls.

There is a red-haired, red-freckled girl called Louise, more my age, that I am friendly with. She comes from some smaller town, not the big city, but her family is spending a week in Montagu at The Baths too. My mother, who, like me, has heard my sister Shulamit's Eartha Kitt record played repeatedly, teases me about Louise by singing the slightly altered words of *Hey Jacque*:

> *Hey, Jacque –*
> *Have you seen Louise?*
> *Is she still in Par-ee?*

One afternoon, when everyone is playing outside, I need to go to the toilet. I walk to one of the WC's at the end of the long outdoor corridor of rooms on the ground level, but it's occupied. Not to worry. A separate room with a bathtub is right next door, and it's empty. I enter, lock the door, urinate in the bathtub and then run the tap to clean it. When I emerge, Louise's mother is right outside and knows immediately that I have not been taking a bath. I am reprimanded.

I don't really care. My love for Louise is merely platonic. My love for Rosa is visceral, but nevertheless pure. I just want her to like me, *a lot*.

One afternoon, I learn the facts of life from some of the older boys. Later that day I tell my mother and Aunt Lizzie, who are chatting in a bedroom, that I know things, and to prove it, I sing the bastardised version of *The Isle of Capri* that the boys taught me:

> *It was on the Isle of Capri where I met her*
> *She was naked and tied to a tree*
> *I couldn't resist the temptation*
> *So now we're a family of three.*

My mother and aunt laugh embarrassedly, but say nothing.

I explain to Leopold that his parents do it, which he refuses to believe. Only other people's parents do that.

Later I hear a crowd of mothers and fathers joking. And then I hear one of the mothers say: "You know the definition of a nymphomaniac? A Jewish woman who goes to bed with her husband the night she's had her hair done."

Now that I've been given a bite of the apple, it's too late. Sex is everywhere.

Chapter 10
Six Moral Tales
Love, Death, and Friendship

THE MAIN CHARACTERS
Howie: a school friend
Gemma: an eleven-year-old girl
Aida: my classmate
Zahava: her younger sister
Harry: an older medical student, will marry Aida
Darren: about my age, will marry Zahava

I. GEMMA 1957

I am twelve years old, the youngest child in Standard 7 (Grade 9). I will be the last to reach puberty, by a long shot – our family custom.

There is a once-a-year Saturday night dance party given by our school, Herzlia, in honour of the twelve-year-old Bat Mitzvah girls. I am invited by Iris, the younger sister of an older classmate. She has to take someone. I am neutral. My mother drives us to the party, dropping us off at the school hall, and will pick us up to go home a few hours later. We are meant to dance to 1950s pop music while the teachers watch from the sidelines.

On the dance floor I see a dark green-eyed flashing girl of eleven from a lower grade, Gemma. (Ten years later, my second year in New York City, I wake up to WNEW one morning to hear that her uncle is the recipient of the first heart transplant.)

We don't have to always dance with the girl we came with. I summon up the nerve to ask Gemma to dance with me. The dance everyone does we called "bopping" – hands never touch each other's bodies, the boy twirls the girl by holding one hand and letting go as she rotates 360 degrees. Out of politeness I regularly ask Iris to dance, but my eye is on Gemma. At 10 pm my mother comes to pick us up; we drop Iris off at her parents' flat and go home. In bed I try to sleep, but all I can think about is Gemma. Eventually I seek some comfort by going to speak to my parents, telling them I can't sleep, but not telling them why.

My best friend is still Howie, and he was at the Bat Mitzvah dance too. He is two years older than me and several years more mature. Soon Gemma is his girlfriend. When he and I first met, his family lived in Oranjezicht and mine in Salt River, which his practical mother had thought was too lower-class for a friend of his. Now I am living in Oranjezicht like Howie, but Gemma, it turns out, still lives in Salt River.

In less than a year, it ends. I never find out why but I suspect it's connected with his practical mother.

2. ZAHAVA 1960

When I was five, my new pretty classmate Aida in Sub B (Grade 2) took the pencil sharpener globe I gave her as a present and said she still didn't like me.

At fifteen, in Standard 9 (Grade 11), I fall in love with Aida's younger sister Zahava, two grades below me. This lasts much longer than any previous infatuation. Like Aida, Zahava is also a round-faced plump pretty girl, prettier and gentler than her sister. She has matured early, more a woman than a girl at thirteen or fourteen, yet she is still puzzlingly angelic looking.

Zahava has juvenile diabetes – everyone knows that she injects her own thigh with insulin daily. She is a good swimmer, winning races in the school's annual swimming gala. More than one of the boys in my class is vainly in love with her, and I'm jealous of anyone who likes her, fearful they will succeed. She casts a spell. One good friend of mine who is also in love with her develops a brain tumour.

When he goes to London for surgery, he runs a postoperative fever so high that they immerse him in ice water. When he returns to Cape Town, he tells me that, while delirious with fever, he apparently repeatedly recited her name.

Though I am sophisticated and knowledgeable and accomplished at school beyond my then 5' 2" height, though I am humorous and have many girl friends in class, though everyone says I am so mature, I am a boy. Everyone in my class is at least a year older, and many of them are two. During my last year in high school, at age sixteen, I reach only 5' 4" and still look boylike. I don't shave. There are younger kids in my neighbourhood that, to my embarrassment, have an adult physiognomy already.

The end-of-year School Dance is for 11th and 12th graders. The 1960 dance is looming and I want to invite Zahava. But Howie likes her and she likes him too. The plot thickens. Unbeknownst to me, a sympathetic friend of mine tries to sound out Zahava on my behalf. He telephones her sister Aida to ask: if Emanuel invites Zahava to the school dance, will she go? Aida quickly calls Howie to warn him to call and invite Zahava before I do. Because if I invite her first and she turns me down, it would then be intolerably rude of her to go with someone else. When I finally call, Zahava tells me she has already been invited.

When the stage musical *Irma La Douce* is produced in Cape Town, Howie and Zahava swoon over *Our Language of Love*: "I'll touch your cheek. I'll hold your hand, and only we will understand, that the silence is broken, in our language of love."

3. HOWIE AND I

Surprisingly, this doesn't much harm the friendship between Howie and me.

We remain best friends all through high school. He comes to my house most afternoons after we do our homework. Groups of my friends collect in the street to play touch rugby, soccer or even cricket. Often, Howie and I stand in the dusk with our hands in our pockets, bouncing up and down on the hilly sloping sidewalk, talking about life and sports and politics, sometimes acting out

Harold-Pinter interactions[24] in which one of us starts to dominate and insult the other verbally and then suddenly, the tables turn and the roles reverse. My mother gives Howie and all my friends her famous homemade cupcakes covered with hundreds and thousands. He often speaks to her about his problems and ambitions.

Outwardly, I behave as though nothing has happened. Inwardly, my sensual imagination is not yet strong enough to make me jealous by thinking of what I might be missing. The capacity to pretend I have not been hurt becomes a pattern in my later life: when someone insults or harms me, I instinctively pretend that I don't notice it, that it doesn't matter, that I have been uninjured, that I am above it. I don't want them to have the pleasure of knowing they have hurt me, even as it rankles. This disguise of injury becomes so essential a part of my nature that I don't realise it's a part of my nature at all. When did this start? Freud would say in the very early years, perhaps when my nanny Marie was sacked. Perhaps earlier?

Howie and I still remain best friends, though our paths diverge after high school. He studies accountancy, articled as an apprentice during the day and taking classes at night. His parents are practical about money and so is he; he gets an allowance for entertainment and clothes and dating, and must manage. I go to university to study maths and physics, am uninterested in business. My parents give me money to spend when I need it.

His mother trains him with instructions. My mother trains me by transmitting her attitudes.

4. O TEMPORA O MORES 1962

Years pass. We live in Puritan (white) South Africa, where the 1960s have yet to arrive. Towards the end of my first year at the University of Cape Town, when I am barely seventeen, my cousin Leopold tells me one Friday evening that "he knows for a fact" that Aida, Zahava's sister, and her boyfriend Harry, a medical student of at least twenty or twenty-one, have slept together. *If you see something, say something.*

24 We must have seen a local production of *The Caretaker*.

I tell Howie about it. Howie tells his girlfriend Zahava. Zahava tells her sister Aida.

One afternoon at home I receive a phone call from Harry himself. Have I been spreading false rumours about him? He is enraged. He will call my parents; he will sue. I stupidly tell him that Leopold had told me about it. He calls Leopold, who, much smarter than I am, denies it. Awaiting Harry's threatened visit to my parents for a day or two, I experience a trembling fear of being caught and unmasked, a frozen heartbeat inside. Time slows; I am guilty, the gallows have been erected, and I am standing on the trapdoor.

Finally, Harry comes over uninvited to speak to my parents. And then miraculously, it gets resolved. My sister Shulamit, twelve years older, chuckles at the whole imbroglio and later remarks that he's so upset because it's probably true. Leopold's mother, my aunt Lizzie, tells my parents that since neither I nor Leopold are liars, I must have hallucinated the whole thing. I have been pardoned but my guilt persists.

Later that year, Howie and Zahava break up. In the long run, that turns out to be a good thing for him. Perhaps this breakup, too, has been instigated by his practical mother.

A few months later, Zahava, now in her second-last year of high school, invites me as her date to her class party in the living room of someone's house. I am still not old enough to drive, only seventeen, and so my mother ferries us back and forth in our Ford Zephyr. Zahava and I dance a bit, talk a bit. At one point, she drinks from a small shot glass of clear liquid, and I ask what it is. Vodka, she says, and then I realise she is kidding; she is diabetic and can drink only water, not even soda. I take her home and drop her at her front door. I am no longer interested. And perhaps a little scared, too.

5. ZAHAVA AND DARREN, 1964–1976

In 1964, Zahava begins to go steady with Darren, the head of *Habonim*. I am not certain I like Darren. He is charismatic and confident and skilled at the skits that pass as entertainment at *Habonim* Saturday night meetings, but he is too forcefully certain that what he is doing personally is right for everyone else. I don't like the unremitting pressure he applies on the rest of us to be like him – to go and live on a kibbutz in Israel – and the scorn he pours on those of us who don't. I am a bit scared of him.

Darren is majoring in sociology at UCT, while I am majoring in physics. Once, when I am preparing to go to New York for a PhD at Columbia, I tell him that I will spend the next few months reading Dirac's *Quantum Mechanics*, a classic textbook filled with difficult maths and physics. "How can it take you months to read a book?" Darren jeers. He cannot conceive of a book that takes months to read and master. He cannot imagine new concepts you have to try to comprehend on each page, formalism that you have to learn, proofs that you have to struggle to understand and make your own. Pointless to explain.

When I leave Cape Town for Columbia in 1966, he and Zahava leave for Kibbutz Tzorah in Israel to live a Zionist Socialist life. On my way to America I visit Israel and see them briefly on Tzorah.

Ten years later, I am a postdoc in the Department of Theoretical Physics at Oxford. My wife is a biology postdoc at Oxford too. We are friendly with two ex-*Habonim* people living in London. Through them we meet up with Darren and Zahava, who are now in London. They have left kibbutz and Darren is studying for a PhD at the London School of Economics. He displays no embarrassment about having left kibbutz, despite his earlier arrogant idealism. That was then, this is now.

In one part of my mind I recognise that people are allowed to change their minds. But I am amazed at how people can be self-righteous for one period, to the point of tormenting those who have different standards, and then simply put their past behind them.

And now Darren and Zahava are divorcing. They tell their children that Mommy and Daddy don't love each other anymore. "Why can't Mommy and Daddy stay together even if they don't love each other?" one of the children asks.

Ten years later Zahava dies, a consequence of diabetes. Six years later, Darren, who has two children with a new wife, has a heart attack and dies too. I learn that he was very active in Zionist politics in London. According to his obituary in an English newspaper,

... he remained an idealist in an age when idealism arouses suspicion. His total refusal to compromise his ideals made his search for suitable employment even more difficult at a time when any such work was in short supply. At the time of his death, despite his rich talents, he was unemployed.

6. FRIENDSHIP 1950 –

Howie and I remain good friends. When I leave South Africa, we go in different directions. Like some other friends of mine there, he probably believes that life in South Africa is enviable and life abroad is harder. And it is.

Ten years later, South Africa's future is less enviable and he and his family emigrate to the US where he becomes a partner at a Big Five accounting firm. He lives in a house in the suburbs of New York City. I continue with physics research, living in university apartments, peripatetically moving to wherever the open academic positions are. Until I get a job at Bell Laboratories, and then, finally, on Wall Street.

Years later, Howie tells me that he thinks about the consequences of every decision he makes. He tells me the strategy he had for choosing a job and a wife. I am suddenly aware that I have no strategy for the most important things in life. I am often impetuous, fueled by the present. Is he really that rational? Is his approach better? I don't know. I admire his practical streak.

He is always gracious and kind, someone to rely on when times are difficult. Many years later, when I have some professional success in finance after leaving physics, he contacts my sisters in Cape Town to congratulate them and make them happy.

Chapter 11
Summertime

One day someone tells me that if you put Sea and Ski suntan lotion on your sixpence it will jam the pinball machine and give you endless games.

In the summer, a Jewish kid's fancy lightly turns to thoughts of Muizenberg.

Every summer we spend two weeks at The Queens Hotel, a dark and shabby three-storey establishment owned by my father's cousins Rivka and Yehuda Iloni.

Rivka was originally a Derman, Uncle *Ephraim-der-Kleiner*'s sister. Many of the Dermans stay there for two weeks in the summer, the only season when it's open. Run by Jews for Jews, it nevertheless has English customs, and so every meal from breakfast to dinner involves baked haddock, and every room has a chamber pot since the shared bathroom is at the end of the corridor or even halfway up another flight of stairs. I sleep in a room with my parents, and they request on a form each night whether they want to have tea or coffee in bed with their biscuits, all delivered on a tray to their room each morning at 6:00 or 7:00 am.[25]

Everyone (white and Jewish) from the southern part of Africa migrates south to summer in Muizenberg for a few weeks. The richer visitors from Johannesburg go to The Balmoral, named after you-know-who's castle. It's fancier, more regal, and more English than The Queens. Rhodesians also come to Muizenberg, but with their better British-sounding accents, they stay at Rhodesia By The Sea. My crowd is wary of the Johannesburgers. The local girls know that the boys from Johannesburg, the big city, are faster than those from Cape Town. Some of them like that.

The water along the long white strand is fabulous for swimming and body surfing, warm by Atlantic standards because of the sheltering surroundings of False Bay. There are many contiguous beaches, each frequented by a different age group. Tubby's Beach opposite The Queens is for families with toddlers; it has swings and slides. Balmoral Beach is for adults. Where the boys and girls my age and older meet is in the Snake Pit, a densely crowded fashionable triangle of white sand sandwiched between the beach boxes and the cement Promenade above. It's packed with white teenage boys and girls on beach towels or in deck chairs.

25 The nature of this apparent adult luxury eludes me now. Why, on your holiday, would you want to have tea or coffee brought to you in bed long before breakfast and then go back to sleep?

The local beaches are for whites only – the more deserted stretch of beach beyond Muizenberg towards Strandfontein is for Coloureds. What Coloureds can do in the Snake Pit is, of course, provide service, wandering up and down selling paper cups of delicious lychees for a shilling. At dusk, when the beach empties out, other groups of Coloured men and women materialise on the white beach to systematically strain the sand through sieves for dropped pennies, tickeys, sixpences, and shillings.

There is a ritual to entering the Snake Pit if you're old enough for the social scene. First, you walk along the Promenade above the Pit and then sit on the cement wall overlooking it, your legs dangling above the beach. You survey the scene, see who is where, decide whom you will join, and only then go down to sit near the people you spotted.

All of Muizenberg's beaches are divided in two by a double row of brightly coloured (red, yellow, blue, or green) wooden bathing boxes that run parallel to the water. Families can rent a semi-detached half of a box for the season; you can lock beach equipment in them, and change in and out of your bathing costume in apparent privacy. We don't have such a box, but two school friends of mine one summer periodically go into their family's half of a box to peek through holes they have surreptitiously poked in the dividing wall in order to watch their attractive girl cousins in the adjacent half changing out of their bathing costumes.

My sister Ruth hangs out in the Snake Pit with all her boyfriends, most of them the fast Johannesburg guys who are down for the season and are hotter properties. I often sit with her circle. She is at university and wears a leopard skin bathing costume and smokes and makes a beauty spot beneath her right eye with an eyebrow pencil. I try one out too.

In the Snake Pit, when I'm ten or eleven, the really cool boys and girls wear thin gold or silver chains with Stars of David around their necks. There is something sexy and shameless and insincere about their wearing the symbol. Still, I want one too, I want that look, but my sisters think it's *prost,* and I know I cannot embarrass myself by asking for one. Some other boys and girls wear silver-linked "identification bracelets" engraved with their name, which they swap to show they are "cased," going steady. I am years away from that, and anyway, the bracelets have a touch of *prost*ness too.

Muizenberg *looks* English, but what drives us is American fashion and American music. The summer when I'm eleven, the hot items are fluorescent socks in lime green or neon pink that glow in the dark as we stroll up and down the Promenade at night. Those strolls are a local version of what my parents call *shpatzieren*, the pre-WWII *Mitteleuropean* slow promenading up and down the main street on a Saturday or Sunday summer afternoon, the men in white suits walking arm-in-arm with their parasol-carrying wives, the men doffing their hats to the opposing women on someone else's arm, the women smiling back in response. Here in the Southern Hemisphere, teenagers and parents *shpatzier* in casual clothes or shorts.

There are lots of sanctioned opportunities for girl-boy stuff. The Muizenberg town council sets up a triangular wooden dance floor on the lawns where, at 4 pm, and sometimes in the evening too, a DJ in a little hut plays through a loudspeaker the latest records, from Bill Haley and the Comets and Tommy Steele to Elvis and Pat Boone. Near-teenage or teenage girls and boys stand around the wooden waist-high rail of the enclosure; you approach a girl and ask her to bop. It takes courage to dance in public view.

The main beach road of Muizenberg has everything you could want. On one very short stretch are shops and cafes and entertainment to fill day and night.

The local bioscope is called The Empire. Its floor is sticky with a thin layer of dried spilled cooldrinks that feel and sound like Scotch tape as your bare feet lift off it. Upstairs is reserved for Coloureds. The Empire shows cowboy films with Roy Rogers and Gene Autry. My cousin Ronnie debates with me endlessly the relative strengths and merits of each of them. I like Gene, he likes Roy better.

Next door, the Maccabi Cafe is run by Tex, a weird moustachioed Portuguese man whom my mother and I later see in Cape

Town centre at OK Bazaars, shoplifting. We avert our eyes rather than turn him in. The Cafe has a large restaurant area and scores of pinball machines that take sixpence for a game. One day someone tells me that if you put Sea and Ski suntan lotion on your sixpence it will jam the pinball machine and give you endless games. I try it, and sure enough, though I don't deserve it from my score, I get free game after free game, collecting a small crowd around me until I leave in fear that I will be caught. The next day the machine is Out of Order. At the back of the restaurant is a staircase that runs up to some other area no one has ever been to. My sister Ruth tells me that people told her there is a brothel upstairs, and I tell my friends. There are indeed occasional men and waitresses mysteriously going up and down.

Fervid romances bloom, full of discussion and passion and the passing of messages through intermediaries between a boy and girl who may like each other. For the first few years, the romances are chaste, devoid of any sexual activity or even desire. A year or two later, the kissing starts.

But it's not all about girls. Between the Promenade and the main street lies a large array of lawns fringed by rockeries, with cement paths between the lawns. It is here where, when I visit Muizenberg, we arrange pick-up games of cricket with the local Muizenberg boys. Someone brings a bat and some stand-up wickets to place on the cement path, the older boys sequentially pick people for the teams, and then we play. Here, too, is where my Muizenberg cousin Alan and I try intensely to hypnotise each other. We believe that it takes a weak will to get hypnotised, and are disappointed when we don't succeed.

Some summers I stay for a week with my cousin Ronnie and Uncle Ephraim and Aunt Jeanette (*Unsere* Jeanette) in their house on Dover Road. The Muizenberg air is salty and their car, like the cars of all the people who live there, quickly becomes spot-rusted on the body and the chassis beneath. During the day we go to the beach with Ronnie's more worldly Muizenberg friends, swim, and try to get as brown as possible with, at most, only olive oil on our skin. There is no such thing as SPF. Some kids are forced by their mothers to wear thick layers of Nivea Cream; very uncool. We go fishing off the concrete embankment at the side of the lagoon that runs from the vlei to the sea, using a hand-held thread of nylon, a hook, and a bit of mussel on the end of it.

Ronnie is a year older than I am, and many years more mature. He is already having experiences that are beyond my ken or desire. One night he takes me with his girlfriend to the sand dunes that run on for miles into the southern distance in the dark at the end of the Promenade, white hollows and mounds just barely visible in the gloom. We settle down in a hollow and he necks with his girlfriend and smokes a cigarette while I sit there quietly. I can see nothing in the dark. When we come back to his house there is ash on his sweater. Auntie Jeanette asks what it is, and he says it's sand and brushes it off. I sleep in the extra bed in his room. Between the sheets is sand that has come off my body and my feet and it rubs against me all night long.

One evening after he and his girlfriend have broken up we go to The Empire bioscope, and on the way he tells me about it, smiles wistfully, and sings *A Certain Smile*:

You love a while and when love goes
You try to hide the tears inside with a cheerful pose.
But in the hush of night exactly like a bittersweet refrain
Comes that certain smile to haunt your heart again.

Nine years later, when I am in New York in 1967, Astrid Gilberto records a bossa nova version, heartless because of the rhythm but sad anyhow.

 Muizenberg is a daytrippers' resort too. When we don't holiday in the hotel or in a rented house, my mother drives us the fourteen miles from central Cape Town to Muizenberg along a narrow two-way road that takes an hour or more in traffic, stopping *en route* to buy trays of peaches or figs or entire watermelons from

roadside vendors. She taps the watermelons skilfully and can tell if they are ripe. My uncle Simcha sometimes drives me and my cousins there in his snazzy white Ford, but insists on pulling over at about the half-way point, thirty minutes into the drive, to take a fifteen-minute nap while we all keep quiet. At lunchtime, we picnic on the Muizenberg lawns. The fancier families, not us, unpack elegant imported English wicker picnic boxes containing neat stacks of English china and sets of bone-handled knives and forks secured by leather toggle straps.

At the centre of Muizenberg is a regal Pavilion with a high dome, and within it a Milk Bar where you can twirl on raised red leather bar seats and order milkshakes or banana splits. Extending from the dome on its left wing is an English-style penny arcade with purely mechanical games. One of them involves dropping a large contemporary copper penny into a slot and onto the tracks of a glass-enclosed vertical wheel, and then rolling the penny progressively down the horizontal tracks by tilting the wheel from side to side without letting it fall off the edge. The prize is getting your penny back. Also inside the arcade is a very small studio where you can pay to have your voice recorded on a small shellac-covered tin disk. That's where my father had me record the little vinyl record. Such a recording plays a pivotal role at the climax of Graham Greene's *Brighton Rock*, and Muizenberg is surely modelled on Brighton or Blackpool.

Roaming everywhere on the beach and Promenade are scattered photographers from Movie Snaps. They wear Movie Snaps T-shirts and carry a 35mm camera with a giant oversized spool for 35mm film. They take your photo, often without your permission, and the next day, you can go to their kiosk on the Promenade, find your photo in their display, and order copies. A similar scheme plays a critical role in *Brighton Rock*.

When we are a little older, Howie and I take the train there from town with an allowance of 2/6 (two shillings and sixpence) for the day. We store our stuff in a locker in the Pavilion. You can get a hot dog and chips and a Coke for a shilling at Norman's, and still have money for playing pinball.

Once, the first summer we live in a rented house rather than a hotel, I am idling alone at the entrance to the Promenade before going home for lunch. An elderly Jewish man approaches me and relates how, when he was thirteen years old, he found the Jewish religion and his Bar Mitzvah preparations unsatisfying and turned to Jesus. He is very convincing, and for a day or two, I worry silently that it might happen to me.

Chapter 12
The Unmentioned

Imprisoned by the British, killed by the Germans.

There is a brother my father mentions only once or twice in my life. His name is Yisroel. Occasionally my father or one of the other brothers might say his name in passing in a Yiddish conversation, but he's almost never alluded to. My mother, though, once tells me quasi-secretly how, after she married my father and came to live in Slonim, a man showed up at the front door one day and announced that he was my father's brother. She hadn't been told about him.

Eventually I decipher most of the story through my Israeli cousin Ora.

Yisroel (Israel) Dereczynski was the eldest of the brothers, born in 1896 or perhaps 1898. His father sent him from Slonim to Palestine as a young teenager to study at the Hebrew Teachers Seminary, and to scout out the possibility of emigration for everyone else in the family. I've read bits of letters from his parents to him written during his first year in Jerusalem, in Hebrew from his father Menahem, in Yiddish from his mother Henye Leah.

In Jerusalem, Yisroel is alone, has health problems, and is short of money, which his parents try to send him, together with local newspapers, via travellers from Slonim to Palestine. Mail takes perhaps a month.[26] When his father dies around 1912, he officially takes the patronymic name Yisroel Ben-Menahem.

When Turkey enters World War I, more than 11,000 Jews are deported from Palestine to Egypt, Yisroel among them. A teenager

---

26 Having been very lonely and isolated myself when I came to New York fifty years after Yisroel went to Jerusalem, with only snailmail access to my friends and family at home, my heart hurts for him.

alone, he suffers through a very tough time in Alexandria for five years, making what living he can as a Hebrew teacher.

In 1919, after the British take over Palestine, he returns to Jerusalem. In June 1920 he is incarcerated in Acre gaol with members of the Haganah, to which he apparently belongs. The photos he sends from jail to his family in Slonim show Yisroel in a white jacket, elegant, homeless, and familyless. The man sitting in front of him, in the group photo, as far as I can tell, is Ze'ev Jabotinsky.

Yisroel. The Hebrew handwriting says: "This is me."

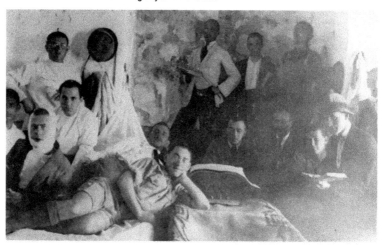

Yisroel in a white jacket in the centre, in Acre Prison.

Next he travels to New York. A letter in 1920 from the Zionist Organization of America introduces him to someone at Jewish Theological Seminary so that he can study Semitic languages. I cannot find out how he got there and who paid for it.

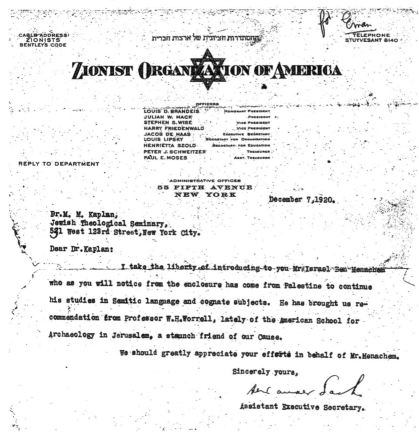

From there the trail peters out and ends badly: vague unconfirmed stories of him living in NYC with a family, disapprovingly infatuated with their daughter, psychologically unwell, fearing once again that he is being sought by the British authorities.

Most likely he returns to Slonim to his mother, who, by then having received permission to emigrate to South Africa, leaves him to be looked after by a village woman to whom she sends money. And then, of course, come the Germans and the destruction of the Jews of Slonim *en masse*.

His siblings in Cape Town rarely speak of him because of the guilt of having left him behind.

I have a framed certificate from the Jewish National Fund commemorating his inscription into their Golden Book as a member of the Haganah and a prisoner at Acre.

Chapter 13
School's Out

In 1954 Roger Bannister breaks the four-minute mile running on the Iffley Road track at Oxford. It's a bit unfair – he has Chris Chataway and Chris Brasher as pacers who take him through each quarter.

By the time I'm eight, I am old enough to take the bus from Oranjezicht to town alone, to OK Bazaars. It's exciting. My mother gives me 2/6 to secretly buy, all by myself, a birthday present for her. I pick out a brooch: a gold-coloured ring with a turquoise bird suspended in the middle. I'm proud of my good taste.

READING

We read mostly English series-books – the *Biggles* WWII adventures, the *Just William* series about William and the Outlaws. WWII seems very recent to us. Howie and I think the following is really funny, capable of being repeated many times without loss of humour:

> William to his father: *When will I be getting a car?*
> Mr Brown: *Not while I'm alive.*
> William, after a pause: *How soon after you're dead?*

We devour the Teddy Lester boarding school books, which seem to be set in the 1950s. Years later, I discover that they were written around 1910, but because they are set in the countryside rather than the city, there are no anachronisms that make them seem out of date. I read the Hardy Boys and also, guiltily and with pleasure, Nancy Drew.

I get *Tiger*, a weekly magazine from England, full of boys' sports adventures.

But one of the girls in my neighbourhood, Sandra, subscribes to *Girls' Crystal*, the girls' equivalent of *Tiger*, mailed weekly from England. She lends me one and I become absorbed in one of the adventures in that issue, to be continued, and ask my mother and father to get me a surreptitious subscription. I don't want anyone to see *Girls' Crystal* lying around if they come to our house.

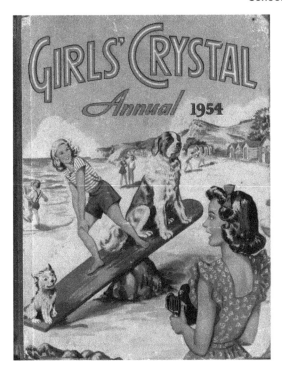

ROAMING

On the slopes of the mountain near our house is the pipe track –
thick black water pipes a foot or more in diameter running like
a Roman road six or more feet above the ground, carrying water
around the peninsula. I like to try to tightrope-walk where the
pipes are not too high above the ground, balancing on them for
short distances. I imagine I'm really good at it.

Nearby is an old quarry, a deep chasm in the mountain whose entrance is hard to find. The local rifle club uses it for target practice and you can hear the shots echoing off the walls. When they are gone we go in and collect *doppies*, the empty cartridges. If you half cover the top with two thumbs and blow over it, there is a piercing whistle.

MODEL KITS

When I go to town alone I regularly visit the Jack Lemkus hobby shop on St George's Street to buy balsa wood plane kits. Some kits are too difficult for my patience and skills, requiring days of careful assembly, but others, the simple gliders, are too unsatisfyingly easy to piece together, taking only a few minutes. It takes experiment to find the level of ambition that is both interesting and fulfillable.

The only plane I successfully complete is a Zippy, which my cousin Abner builds too. It takes great care and patience, and days of work. The kit contains long thin strips of lightweight balsa for the frame and flat sheets with preprinted supporting structural inserts that prevent the frame from collapsing. You have to carve and sand a block of balsa for the nose. I pin the plan to my mother's bread-kneading board and then use more pins to force the long balsa strips to curve along the frame's arcs. Finally, I cement the pieces together with airplane glue. The fuselage is translucent tissue paper cemented to the balsa frame, trimmed, then dampened with water so it shrinks taut, and finally, when it's dry, lacquered and painted. The engine is a long rubber band that runs from the nose to a hooked pin at the tail. You rotate the propeller many times to wind up the rubber band and then let it loose. It sort of flies, erratically. Abner, two years older, follows the instructions more carefully than I do, sanding off any excess glue on the frame before overlaying the tissue. His looks much better.

I am not, and never will be, a good experimentalist or engineer.

SPORTS

The neighbourhood boys congregate on our street on school-day afternoons and weekends. Cars come by but cede the right of way to us. We play until dark – touch rugby and soccer with small teams in the winter, cricket with a tennis ball in the summer. We go out barefoot when it's warm. Sometimes we take our wickets and bat and cork ball to the nearby Gardens Rugby Club grounds and play cricket there.

The cork ball has a moulded ersatz seam. A leather ball with a genuine sewn seam would be great but that's too expensive and, even more significantly, too pretentious. You have to be talented to deserve one of those.

I play cricket for our school's Under-12's against other schools. It's primitive: we don't wear gloves[27], and I get my thumb smashed against the bat by another school's fast bowler. I go on painfully batting for a few more balls until I'm out.

At the Gardens Tennis Club lower down on Molteno Road there are red clay courts. I take tennis lessons, serving with a box of 100 balls until I get it right. Somehow the lessons stop before I get to backhand, leaving me with a life-long deficit. The most envied rackets have real animal-gut strings. If the racket is left in the rain

---

27 These are the days long before helmets are worn, even in professional cricket.

or dew, the gut shrinks when it dries and you need a tennis press to prevent the frame from warping.

We debate the merits of Dunlop vs. Slazenger. Almost everyone wants a Dunlop Maxply, as do I, and eventually my mother buys me one for £5. The woodwork is a triumph of craftsmanship and art.[28]

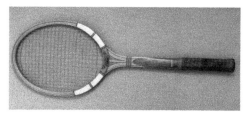

INSPIRATION

In May 1954 Roger Bannister breaks the four-minute mile on the Iffley Road track at Oxford. It's a bit unfair – he has Chris Chataway and Chris Brasher as pacers who take him through each quarter at the appropriate pace. It doesn't seem right.

28 I still used it 20 years later to play tennis (on grass) at Oxford in the late 1970s, and in New York in the early 80s.

Bannister is not a professional runner; he's a working doctor. A month or two later Australian John Landy breaks Bannister's world record. But Bannister beats him, though not his world record time, in their meeting at the Empire Games that summer. This is legendary stuff and we know all the details. The iconic photo is an inspiration to us all.

To emulate him, my friend Max and I time ourselves for two laps around the local reservoir on the street where Max lives. We are sure, somehow, that two laps make a mile, and we practise often. At other times I pace out 100 yards on the flat road above the orphanage and then run 17.6 times up and down the length of road with a stopwatch borrowed from my sister Ruth. She uses it to administer IQ tests in the Child Guidance Clinic where she works.

LA TRAVIATA

I'm not exposed to much culture: virtually no classical music at home, no literary classics given to me to read. My friends and I read whatever boy books are popular. One afternoon though, when I'm no more than ten years old, our school takes us to the grand Victorian-style Cape Town City Hall, opposite the Grand Parade, to see *La Traviata*.

When Violetta dies of tuberculosis, I suddenly start to think of how one day my parents will be dead and I will be alone in the world.

JIU JITSU

I am eight when my mother's sister Yafa comes to visit from Tel Aviv, where she lives on Allenby Street. She works at *Kupat Holim* as a pharmacist, but we have photos of her in her dapper khaki uniform with the British Army in Egypt during the war. She might have been part of the *Auxiliary Territorial Service*. From Egypt she would send packets of military-issue Wrigley's gum by sea mail to my sisters, four crisp white sugar-coated little lozenges to a packet. It was wartime in South Africa, and they chewed gum as a treat during the day and stored it in a glass of water at their bedside at night, so as to reuse it the next day.

Yafa is a very good sport. I have a green coarse-leaved illustrated paperback book on *The Art of Jiu-Jitsu* that I study, and she lets me practise hip-throwing her on our front lawn. She helps me change water to wine with my chemistry set and phenolphthalein.

Yafa is the one unconventional sister of my mother's. A few years later she begins to live with Julek, a formerly or perhaps still married man. There is something mysterious and unspoken about the whole business. He collects Israeli art, and later, they send my wife and me a delicate painting of a vase of flowers.

When I visit Israel in the early sixties I usually stay with Naomi and her family, and hang out with my favourite Israeli cousin Rivka.[29] But for a night or two, to be equitable, I go and stay with Yafa and Julek. When I do, they carefully and ostentatiously go to sleep in different bedrooms, surely for my benefit. My father, who has a twist of severe prudishness running through him, once, arguing with my mother, tells her that Yafa is immoral.

One of Shulamit's friends, a roué who has had many consecutive and parallel affairs during his life, even through his 80s, remarks to us in the early 1970s, while Yafa is visiting my ill mother in Cape Town, that "Yafa is a very attractive woman." And he's a connoisseur.

29 She and I kid around a lot. If I get mock angry, she asks me if I'm *broiges*, an old-fashioned beautiful Yiddish word for a kind of sulking petulant anger, a word that I recognise but hardly ever hear.

Chapter 14
La Vie En Rose, Part I

These are my idea of sophistication – memories of The Long Fifties which ran from 1950 through 1963 when Kennedy was assassinated.

JULIETTE GRECO! EDITH PIAF! EARTHA KITT! AMALIA SINGING FADO AT THE OLYMPIA!

Ten years old in 1955, I am too young for these songs, but I am opened up to them when my sister Shulamit returns from abroad. I don't remember much about her before she left for Europe after three years at the University of Cape Town. At about nineteen, twelve years older than me, she says she was too busy with her own adolescence to pay me much attention. One rare early recollection from age four is going with my mother to pick her up at university, waiting beside our car on University Drive for her to emerge from the crowds of students. I walk up to one of them and ask "Have you seen Shulamit?" and then I realise that in this crowd, that name does not define her. Another memory is going to visit her friend Becky Lan in Pinelands. I watch them prepare to bake cakes, and am allowed to dip my finger in the delicious raw sugary batter and lick it.

England, and "the continent" as everyone in colonial South Africa calls it, is where young people go postwar. Shulamit leaves when I am about seven, and we see her off at the Cape Town docks on a Union Castle liner to Southampton. People send flowers and bowls of fruit to her cabin – that's how you saw people off in those days on those ships. In London, where she has some friends, she finds a job as a social worker for a year or two. Then she goes to work in Tel Aviv where we have relatives. She works with tuberculosis patients and often fears that she is catching TB herself.

From England she sends me a grand magician set with a wand and cape and tricks you can do, and two pairs of genuine leather boxing gloves. In our still small Jewish school that tries to ape the extracurricular activities of the tougher gentile schools, some boys actually take boxing as a sport, instructed by Mr Purchase who has one genuine cauliflower ear from being punched too much. The school holds a one-night-a-year boxing evening, attended by parents and children, in which boys of similar weight fight three rounds with each other. My tough eleven-year-old classmate Charles Rosenthal cries while he continues to batter his opponent and is battered in return, punching while tears stream down his face. How do parents allow their children to do this? Luckily I wear glasses and cannot box at school. But with Shulamit's boxing gloves I do spar sometimes for a few minutes with Carl Snitcher, one of the older boys in my neighbourhood, a boy who really does know how to box. (His father, Harry Snitcher QC – Queen's Counsel in British Commonwealth parlance – was on the central committee of the Communist Party of South Africa until 1948.) We "fight" in Carl's backyard and he quickly penetrates my defences and chips one of my teeth with a blow to the jaw. He has quickly destroyed my confidence that I can be good at anything. Slowly, but certainly, the recollection of the lesson fades.

When Shulamit returns to Cape Town a few years later she brings back with her the exotic cultural accoutrements of burgeoning European and Israeli life: Eartha Kitt records, Amalia singing fado at the Olympia, avocado dip (which I much later discover is called guacamole), hummus, tahina, espresso, steak which she broils bloody in the toaster oven (I hate the żyła, as my parents call it, Yiddish-Polish for the sinewy part of the meat).

And simultaneously, Cape Town begins to sprout pizzerias, gelaterias, Italian trattorias and Italian films that Shulamit and her friends go to. She is a social worker at *Child Life* in Queen Victoria Street not far from the centre of town. After work ends at 5 pm, she meets her friends at the Negrita coffee shop – such a sophisticated name – in nearby St George's Street. Sometimes she takes me along. Years later when I visit Nice and see the Hotel Le Negresco on the Promenade des Anglais, with its pink dome allegedly inspired by the breast of the architect's mistress, I think of the Negrita. At the Negrita they smoke and talk and drink espressos and eat toasted sandwiches. That's the life I aspire to.

My friends envy me my access to the world of my older sisters: the political-cultural world of Shulamit, the academic child-psychology world of Ruth. I listen to Eartha Kitt on vinyl singing *The Heel* and *Hey Jacque* and *I Want To Be Evil* and *Mambo de Paree* and *The Day That The Circus Left Town*, and to Amalia singing *Barco Negro*. Shulamit belongs to (the intellectual) Film Society which shows uncommercial foreign films on a Sunday night in a cinema that would otherwise be closed, and eventually I start going too. These are my idea of sophistication, and they become the visions of my friends too. They are recollections of The Long Fifties which ran from 1950 through 1963, when Kennedy was assassinated. It was only afterwards that The Sixties began, and they were short.

Chapter 15
La Vie En Rose, Part 2

*Even mind-your-own-business people like us, who dislike but
don't actively oppose apartheid, imagine we can be raided by the
security police.*

My two sisters, twelve and nine years older than me, are very close
to each other, devoted, but too fiercely close.[30] My mother likes to
claim that on the phone she cannot tell which one is which. But
they are different.

1942

Ruth, the younger one, has been the easy daughter who excels at
university, wins medals for the best student in anthropology and
psychology, has lots of boyfriends during the summer at the Snake

---

30 Seeing them argue when they are in their seventies, I tell them they should
get divorced, and they laugh and say I have hit the nail on the head.

Pit. She has taught me to read and write early. She recites aloud to me *The Rime of the Ancient Mariner* as she studies high school poetry, reels off facts about the Industrial Revolution to me as she reviews history, informs me about Eli Whitney's cotton gin and the spinning jenny. She reads me George Bernard Shaw's *St Joan* and *Androcles and the Lion*, using me as an audience while she reinforces her knowledge and provides my education. Later, when she's at university, she tells me about Margaret Mead and *Coming of Age in Samoa*. She practices her clinical work by giving me countless IQ and personality tests with a stopwatch that I sometimes borrow to time my mile runs.

Sometimes her nurturing goes too far. I receive a prize in school in Standard Three at age nine for a long multi-page report we have to write at home, over several weeks, on the topic of Travel. I don't have a clue about how to prepare a systematic account of travel through the ages, but Ruth makes it her project, groups it into Land, Sea, and Air sections, finds the appropriate pictures in magazines from which she cuts out illustrations, and then dictates to me, sentence by sentence, what to write, which I resentfully do. When I tire she occasionally forges my handwriting for a few figure captions. Is it her ambition for me that drives her to have me submit a plagiarised report? And what possesses me to go along with it?

Shulamit, twelve years my senior and now back in Cape Town after several years in England and Israel, is the bohemian daughter as far as my parents are concerned. On the one hand, she is a social worker; all the members of our extended family who need help or psychological advice consult her. One uncle and aunt have a child with Down syndrome, and Shulamit helps with finding and applying for services. On the other hand, she isn't married and, for my parents, this is a problem that intensifies as time passes.

She works for the *Child Life* organization. Driving the small classic Morris Minor they let her use, she visits cases in the poor Coloured neighbourhoods or on the desolate sand dunes of the Cape Flats where the government has forcibly relocated non-white residents of central Cape Town.

Shulamit has interesting friends: Ida and Walter; Miriam Green – the daughter of Mrs Schwartz who supposedly saved my life by feeding me when I had bronchitis as a newborn – and her husband Harry; Albie Sachs, the anti-apartheid lawyer who later becomes a Constitutional Court judge in the new South Africa; Ronnie Segal, who edits the anti-apartheid *Africa South* magazine which is soon banned by the Nationalist government, and who will have to go into exile. At my Bar Mitzvah celebration, when we give Ronnie a lift from synagogue to the luncheon, he tells us that his mother bemoans his political activities, which she says will drive her to an early grave, to which he replies that at her age it's much too late for that.[31]

When the Nationalist government starts to clamp down on anti-government protests in the early 1960s, when the underground African Resistance Movement led by the aptly named ex-*NUSAS* president Adrian Leftwich is committing sabotage to protest the apartheid regime, the government puts Albie in jail without trial under the Emergency Act, for 180 days, with only a Bible to read. Shulamit and her friends take turns bringing home-cooked meals for Albie to the Roeland Street jail each evening, to be given to him by the wardens. Eventually released without ever having been charged, he runs non-stop from jail all the way to Clifton Beach to swim in the ocean. When he works on writing *The Jail Diary of Albie Sachs*, and fears that if he is arrested again he will lose his manuscript, my mother, I believe, keeps a copy locked in her bedroom wardrobe with her shoebox of letters and other mementos

---

31 Gideon Shimoni in *Community and Conscience: The Jews in Apartheid South Africa*: "... the apparent paradox that while many whites who actively opposed apartheid were Jews, few Jews were active opponents of apartheid."

of her parents. Our old copies of *Africa South* she fearfully buries in the back garden. Even mind-your-own-business people like us, who dislike but don't actively oppose apartheid, imagine we can be raided by the security police. We admire Albie's courage and consistency, from a distance.

Albie becomes a good family friend, has meals with us some evenings, advises me on careers, helps me edit an essay about my goals when I apply to study overseas for a Ph.D. In 1966 he goes into exile in London from South Africa. Later, while living in Maputo in 1988, he loses an arm and the sight in one eye when his car is bombed by South African security agents.

After her return from England and Israel, Shulamit lives "at home" again, just like most unmarried (white) people in Cape Town in the late 1950s. It must be strange for someone who has been independent. She has her own bedroom, with a single bed and a built-in bedside table and reading lamp as part of the headboard. Next to it is a white plastic bedside radio. Sometimes in the evening we all listen to *Kol Zion LaGolah*, the Israeli radio broadcast to Jews "in the diaspora."

Her long-term boyfriend Mervyn lives on Beach Road, Sea Point, in a flat with his widowed mother. I like Mervyn. He smokes Viceroy cigarettes, plain, cork-tipped. His index and middle finger are slightly nicotine-stained. He buys packs of fifty cigarettes, the flat cardboard box as large as a paperback, green on the front for cork-tipped no filter, red for filter, both of them blank white on the back. He uses the back as a Filofax to keep track of all his notes, ideas, and to-do's, transferring and modifying the list from an empty pack he has finished to a fresh pack he buys. It's cool.

Mervyn is a medical rep for Sandoz, marketing drugs to doctors. But he is also a tremendously skilled photographer who develops, prints, and enlarges all his own pictures. He makes 16 mm films for which he writes the script and then gets all of their friends to act in. He holds evenings where he screens the films. My favourite is a version of the German Expressionist film *The Cabinet of Dr Caligari* with Shulamit's friends in the main roles, complete with titles and cast, and a Script Girl credit for her.

Mervyn has lots of time for me. He shows me how to build an electrostatic sparking machine using two empty tin cans through which drops of water pass (*Kelvin's Thunderstorm*).

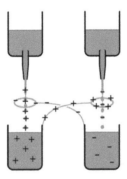

Later he leaves the rep business and becomes a commercial photographer with his own studio, where he takes a photo shoot of me to produce my university graduation photos.

In December of 1958, when I am thirteen, Shulamit and Mervyn take a trip up Africa to Zanzibar. I know that my parents don't like it – this is Fifties' Cape Town. While they are away, my mother, my father, and I vacation for two weeks as usual at The Queen's Hotel in Muizenberg. Meanwhile, Ruth stays with our aunt *Unsere Jeanette* in Muizenberg, and is going out with Paul. He too, after several years in England, is now living at home with his parents even though he is in his late 20s. Early one morning Ruth bursts into our room at the hotel to announce that he proposed. They will marry the following June. The contrast with Shulamit away with Mervyn is unspoken.

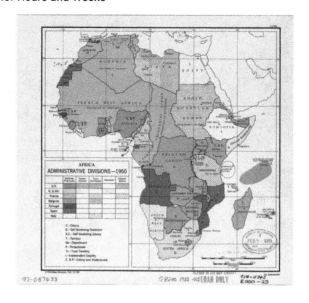

Shulamit and Mervyn continue going out for several years. Late at night he brings her back home in his car, and they sit parked outside our house in Woodburn Crescent for hours. It reminds me then of Marjorie Morningstar, who, no matter how large a part of the night she spends with Noel Airman, always comes home to spend the last few hours in her mother and father's apartment in the Eldorado on Central Park West. (Everything I knew about New York when I moved here I had learned from Herman Wouk's *Marjorie Morningstar*, and it was accurate.)

My friend Howie asks me one day why Shulamit and Mervyn don't marry. Pretending to be broadminded, I reply that it's OK to keep going out together without getting married if you don't want to. I don't really believe it. I know this is just an excuse for something not quite right, but he accepts my worldly analysis.

One day they announce to us that they will marry and Mervyn comes over for Sunday lunch to our house. Everyone kisses and congratulates. I can still feel those kisses on my lips.

Chapter 16
La Vie En Rose, Part 3: Da Capo Al Fine

The rabbi says that we always ask why bad things happen but never stop to ask why good things happen.

In a few short weeks the congratulations lead to nothing. As best I can tell, for I'm still a child, Shulamit calls it off. Something doesn't work for her; perhaps she feels stifled in some way. She doesn't want to marry him.

And so, eventually, it ends. Shulamit, close to thirty in the early 1960s, finally moves out of our family house to share an apartment with two women friends in Sea Point. For my father it's a catastrophe, *a charpah un a neshande* (a shame and a disgrace), an embarrassment almost beyond toleration to have a single daughter who chooses to live not at home but in a flat of her own.

My parents have seen *Butterfield 8* on a Saturday night, and one day I hear my father reminding my mother how, late in the film, Elizabeth Taylor's mother slaps her face, to which she replies, "You should have done that a long time ago."

Whereas Ruth, when she marries in 1959, gets new furniture, linens, an entire *trousseau*, Shulamit furnishes her apartment with second-hand couches and beds. She accepts it – the convention is that certain accoutrements are for women who marry. But it hurts her that there is something second-rate about the way she will live. It is, in all likelihood, my father's fault. My father loves Shulamit, who, among all his children, is most like him, but he is angry at her lifestyle. He thinks, I suppose, that it's a matter of her will. And she loves him and is tremendously proud of his achievements, defending him to everyone until his death and then until her own.

And so she lives in Joubert Road in a shared flat with her friends. I visit there often and she, of course, comes to see us at home all the time. I spend time at her flat too, sometimes studying there. She has new boyfriends, some of them *shaegetzes*[32], whose relationships she hides from my parents, though Ruth and I and Paul know about it and sometimes see her riding in a convertible with one of them as we *shpatzier* on the Sea Point beach front. Her career progresses well; she manages casework at *Cape Mental Health*, she teaches social work at the University of South Africa, she gets deeply involved in organising social services for the elderly in the Jewish community, she is the go-to person for many friends and members of the extended family who have psychological or social issues. She does lots of good for people. Eventually she buys her own apartment on Sea Point beachfront and lives there.

A pipe dream: Perhaps her life would have been better had she not returned to Cape Town from her two or three years in London and Tel Aviv when she was young.

Sometimes I think she wishes she could leave again, but now, settled into Cape Town, she finds it too difficult to make the break anew. Like her siblings and parents, she has separation anxiety, and it's worse for the first-born. Perhaps that is why she encourages me to go abroad to study for a PhD, to make me obtain a quantum of freedom that she didn't attain. Perhaps she fears for what might happen if I stay in my parents' nest.

Nevertheless, long departed from Cape Town, I still carry my parents' voices inside me, their idea of a well-structured life that is *eidel* and not *prost*.

In my fourth year at the University of Cape Town, doing a B.Sc. Hons in applied maths, I realise that serious physics students are applying to do a Ph.D. overseas. I am nothing if not serious and

---

32 *shaegetz* is Yiddish for a non-Jewish young man, the male equivalent of *shiksa*, often used disparagingly.

ambitious, and so I begin to do the same. Shulamit and her friend Albie help me write letters of purpose for scholarship applications, letters in which I say with sincerity that I want to spend my life investigating the laws of the universe.

LA VIE MOINS ROSE

By 1970 when I am married and living in New York and struggling through my PhD, my mother in Cape Town doesn't feel well. Her arms are weak, she says, she has trouble lifting them. Shulamit and Ruth are passionate about my mother and father, and passionately anxious. They take her from doctor to doctor. One neurologist – I have the typewritten letter – writes a sarcastic report back to our general practitioner, Dr Berelowitz,[33] that there is nothing physiological about my mother's feeling of weakness, and that the cure would be to have *her daughter*s get psychiatric therapy.

But eventually, after no success with either diagnosing or eliminating her weakness, my mother does see a psychiatrist, and it is he, the engineer of souls, who recognises the truth about her material body, and sends her for nerve conduction tests, which confirm *ALS*. This is the bell that tolls for Shulamit and Ruth, who frantically look after her for years as she deteriorates, as she first loses the use of her arms, then her legs, until eventually she has trouble swallowing and keeping her neck upright. It takes nine years to culminate.

My mother hates being dependent, hates having an aide to look after her, cannot understand why, as the doctors tell her, her "muscles don't work."

"I didn't even know I had muscles," she says, conflating muscles with the "muscles" of body builders.

She is stoic and does not complain much. Her ailment is a mystery to her, a mystery that never disappears and slowly worsens. No one tells her the diagnosis or prognosis, and really, what's the difference, whatever you call it? It's incurable. When I hear about it in 1971 I rush to the medical library at Columbia and am terrified at what I read. I visit her every summer and meet her in Israel

33 See the following chapter.

when she travels there with Ruth to see her sisters at the start of her illness, while she is still mobile. From America I send her various new experimental drugs, but none of them work. I send her a Spenco gel cushion to help prevent wheelchair bedsores. I send her a device that converts her phone receiver into a speakerphone so that she can talk without having to hold the phone to her ear, which she can no longer do. These are the years before easy and cheap telephoning from New York to South Africa, and so, when she cannot write any more, I send her tape cassettes with my voice descriptions instead of written letters. She replies similarly. I visit there every summer until finally, while I am on vacation in 1979 in the Bahamas with my wife and two-year-old son, she dies, and I fly back.

The rabbi at her funeral says that we always ask why bad things happen but we never stop to ask why good things happen.

My sisters now devote a major part of their life to looking after my father. We are not the kind of children to put parents in homes, or at least my sisters are not, since it is they who bear the brunt of all this. When my mother dies my father goes to live with Ruth and her family. Every morning he gets up and, with his brief case and in his sports jacket, takes the bus from Sea Point to Cape Town to his office. Shulamit and Ruth are now dedicated to helping my father. He has been in a business battle with his swindler brother Simcha, and my sisters take over the battle and fight it to its conclusion, which is resolved not long after my father dies in 1985.

When Shulamit turns 60 in 1993 I send her David Halberstam's book *The Fifties*. She's the link to that decade of cultural and artistic growth in Europe, the link to the films and plays and books and food and social life that formed me.

Chapter 17
The Transmigration of Souls

In Edinburgh as a young man, he realised that if he didn't partake of sexual activity the ability might fade. And so, he says, while there he became a "sexual virtuoso."

Dr Harry Berelowitz is our family doctor all the years I live in Oranjezicht. His house is in nearby Forest Road, his office in town. When he makes house calls – you can call him at any time, even in the middle of the night – he arrives in a little grey chug-chug-chug Austin, carrying a worn black leather bag which contains:

- his stethoscope;
- his dim miner's lamp that he wears on his forehead, connected by wire to a large battery pack in his trousers pocket;

- some wooden sticks to hold your tongue down; and
- a small leather-covered metal case containing a glass syringe and needle that my mother boils in a pot on the stove before he uses it.

In one ear he wears a single-earphone hearing aid, connected by wires to a similarly large battery pack in his jacket pocket. I wonder now how well he could have heard with it.

He has strong bony diagnostic fingers, essential for doctors when the only way of looking inside you is via a blood test or an X ray that takes days to develop and read.[34] He curls his fingers hard into your belly, taps on your chest and abdomen, and feels the resistance or listens to the sounds and makes deductions. He will come to your bedside rain or shine, day or night. When my thumb is smashed by a cricket ball in an inter-school match at age ten, he arrives at night to pierce the nail and let the pressurised blood out. When I have my appendix removed the same year, he is the anaesthetist. When my father has a bout of prostate trouble after I have moved abroad, my mother calls Dr Berelowitz in the middle of the night to insert a catheter. She explains to people that my father's pain was so great that, "you know how he is," he wasn't even ashamed to be examined in front of her.

Once, playing Batman while hanging from a tree branch in the garbage-strewn field across the street, I bat-jumped down and crouched on the ground. Then I looked at my right hand: there was blood pouring from the fleshy part at the base of my thumb. I ran back home crying and my mother pushed cotton wool into the cut and she and Shulamit drove me down to Berelowitz's office in town. There, while they held me down, he poured alcohol into the wound and stitched it.

Dr Berelowitz looks meticulous, precisely put together, a bit frail. His wife is big-boned and younger and refers to him in conversation as "Berelly." She has a square jaw and looks a bit like an

---

34 Now, in 2024, physicians who want the results of a digital X-ray or CT scan or MRI quickly, ask to be given a "wet read," metaphorically referring to long ago when X-rays were developed and handed to the doctor while still covered in wet fixer.

older version of *The Woman in Gold* in the Neue Galerie. She and Berelly look mismatched. She is social, talks a lot, plays cards.

He isn't that way. He is smaller, measured, serious, thoughtful, intellectual, a thin old man with a round bald head and a small residual fringe of white hair at the back. In Muizenberg at the Snake Pit, his family rents a bathing box by the year, and I see him there on summer weekends. After bathing in the sea he emerges from the cold water with his thin legs sticking out of the loose worn-out elasticised Speedo-style bathing briefs that don't keep everything securely in place. He flaps his arms back and forth to recover from the cold water, like an Olympic swimmer warming up at the edge of the pool before the race. No one snickers at his revealing bathing suit; it is merely a foible, like Einstein's wild hair or socklessness.

Berelly is almost twenty years older than my parents, but, through his experience, he is not as foreign as they are. He emigrated to South Africa at the age of 18 in 1907, from Lithuania. "Six weeks after my arrival," he wrote later, "I got a job in a general store in Willowmore, a village in the Karoo. I studied in my spare time, saved every penny, and by 1914 was able to go to the University of Edinburgh and get my degree in 1919." Now he has an

Anglicised accent, with just a touch of careful precision and a hint of foreignness in his diction.

In addition to being a GP, he is an anaesthetist. In the 1920s Berelly worked at the university hospital and was one of the pioneers of modern anaesthetic methods in Cape Town. This was before anaesthetists became specialists and began to take over the field. Once, on being queried on his status, Dr Berelowitz took great delight in stating, "No, I am not a specialist, I am an expert." When I was ten and had my appendix removed, he put me under. During the Israeli War of Independence in 1948, he went to work in Israel as a medic, and helped train anaesthetists there.

As I get into my late teens, Berelly becomes an occasional confidant. Unlike most of the adults I know, he is someone I can talk to about really personal things. When I am about to go abroad to study, he tells me about his sensual life by way of giving me advice. In Edinburgh as a young man, he says, he realised that if he didn't partake of sexual activity the ability might fade, and so, he says, while there he became a "sexual virtuoso." Before I leave Cape Town in 1966, he cautions me to avoid a certain South African professor in New York whose address someone had given me, noting that the man is not suitable company for me. Much later I realise that this was a warning that the professor was gay. That was then.

Whenever I return to South Africa I visit Berelly to catch up. I send him an aerogram occasionally, show him my first published paper while I'm in graduate school. I still have letters he wrote back to me.

When Berelly becomes terminally ill in 1973, I am back home for the summer and go to visit him one last time. In bed and wearing a colostomy bag, he remarks conversationally to me and the other visitors that someone had told him that when you die you meet all your old acquaintances, and he hopes that will be so. He isn't insistent, merely suggesting possibilities.

When my mother comes down with ALS, Berelly is her general doctor, though her treatment, or lack of it, is managed by specialists. We can see that he is saddened by her ten-year-long decline and end after witnessing her earlier beauty and spirit through medical ups and downs.

There is one time he misdiagnoses me. I am eleven and grow weak and ill and nauseated, and no one can figure out what is wrong with me. I am certain that I have polio, now spreading around Cape Town, but I don't tell anyone. I worry silently. Berelly makes a home visit and prescribes chloromycetin, a new antibiotic. When I still don't improve, he runs a blood test that reveals a very low white cell count. Knowing that chloromycetin can cause leukaemia as a rare side effect, he concludes that I have chloromycetin-induced leukaemia. There is a hubbub around my bed which I am aware of without knowing any of these details. Eventually a specialist, Dr Mirvish, comes to my bedside. He quickly realises from another blood test that Berelly has erred and that I merely have glandular fever/mononucleosis. Shulamit remarks that this is the first time she has ever seen Berelly defer to anyone. He gives me a series of Vitamin B injections and I quickly recover. (I vomit several times during the illness and haven't vomited since 👆.)

People like Berelly no longer exist – a doctor who treats you with affection and seriousness, with patience, without patronisation and without superiority, someone who removes rather than crosses boundaries. When my son is born several years after Berelly's death, I look at his round bald head and am immediately reminded of Berelly himself.

I like to think he has been reincarnated.

Chapter 18
Crimes, Sins, and Misdemeanours

I like the Yom Kippur prayers in which you recite the sins of the past year. I like to mentally acknowledge the ones I can recall having committed.

1. Once, when I am ten, I am arguing with my mother about something while she is driving. She takes her left hand off the steering wheel and puts it on me to calm me down, and I say, "Take your fat hands off me." She is hurt; her hands are not young and shapely any more.

2. In the same year, a second cousin who is pregnant comes to visit my mother, to confide and chat. They sit in the lounge on a sofa. The cousin asks for some matches[35], and my mother sends me to get some. I am not in a good mood, and on re-entering the room with the matches, I stop and toss them to her. My mother makes her throw them back at me.[36]

3. Our house in Oranzejicht has many empty lots around it when we first move in, but slowly they get built on and the whole block fills up. The one directly next to us is first. Soon the Wilkens, a childless middle-aged Afrikaner couple, move into their new house. They are one of the few non-Jewish families on the block. Mr Wilken is a manager at the Afrikaner-run Volkskas Bank. Mrs Wilken is a

---

35 Yes, once upon a time pregnant people smoked.

36 This must be a Jewish or East European superstition, that throwing something at a pregnant woman may provoke a miscarriage, which she can avert by throwing it back.

housewife. Their house, like our Charton, has a name, but it is an Afrikaans one: *Kom Nader* (Come Nearer).

A rainy weekday winter school holidays afternoon in July when I am eleven. In our neighbourhood boys spontaneously aggregate in the street or in each other's houses or flats. No prearrangements or permissions are necessary. I am with my younger Liberace-look-alike friend Gerald Daniels who lives at the middle bend of Woodburn Crescent.

With us is one of The Three L's, Leonard, who lives one street down. He is not really a friend of mine, his parents not friends of my parents. We are bored, it's raining, and we have nothing to do, so we gather in Gerald's bedroom and decide to write an anonymous letter to the Wilkens. Perhaps I dictate it, perhaps I write it, I don't recall, but it's a joint project. We write:

Dear Mr and Mrs Wilken:
How are you both today?
You have a beautiful house, and a nice dog,
Maybe you should change the name of your house from Kom Nader
to Gaan Verder.
P.S. Your husband looks a lot like the man on the Ritmeester cigar box.

Gaan Verder is Afrikaans for Go Farther, a childish inversion. And Mr Wilken does indeed look like the man on the cigar box, whose image we draw on the letter. We do not sign it.

Without a further thought, we go out in the rain and drop the letter in their mailbox, and then do something else.

Two days later, Saturday morning, is my cousin Clark's Bar Mitzvah. At 9:00 we are preparing to go to Shul for the occasion. It will be a busy weekend with a post-synagogue celebration on Saturday, a subsequent visit to Simcha and Lizzie's house on Saturday afternoon, and finally a large catered luncheon on Sunday. We are putting on our good clothes for synagogue, jacket and tie for me and my father, dresses and hats for my mother and sisters. Then the doorbell rings.

It is Mrs Wilken who asks my mother if she can come in and speak to her about a letter she found in her mailbox. My mother cannot understand the significance of this and explains that we will be busy with family stuff all weekend, and asks if it can be postponed until Monday. From upstairs I hear Mrs Wilken agree.

The next two days I spend in continuous panic. The noose has been fastened and I am waiting for the chair to be kicked out from under me. I make it through the Bar Mitzvah, I go to the parties, I attend a youth group meeting on Sunday morning, I go to the luncheon on Sunday afternoon, but all the time I tremble inside.

Monday morning Mrs Wilken comes to speak with my mother, who invites her in. Everyone knows that the Wilkens are Afrikaners and Christian, virtually the only gentile house on the block, the only Nationalist Party pro-apartheid supporters in a relatively liberal English-speaking neighbourhood of United Party members. Mrs Wilken explains that a Jewish neighbour across the street saw me drop a letter into their mailbox on the wall in front of her house. She interprets the childishly pencilled letter and childish sentiments, the *Gaan Verder*, as a message from Jews in the neighbourhood that the Wilkens should leave the community. I hear all this from the other room.

I am summoned and admit to everything. I explain that it wasn't just me, but also Gerald and Leonard, but this doesn't matter. No one else is blamed, no one else's parents contacted. I have to go over next door that afternoon to formally apologise to Mrs Wilken. She hugs me. It is all my fault.

It never occurs to me to question the plausibility of her entire backstory. Why would Jewish parents employ a few of their kids to send a message to the Wilkens to leave town? And why would a Jewish neighbour then finger me? Why not regard it as a childish prank and laugh it off and let it go?

On the other hand, when push comes to shove, it is in fact the Wilkens that we sent a letter to, not anyone else.

4. I try to fast on Yom Kippur for the first time when I am twelve, a year earlier than required. Jewish fasting involves absolutely no

eating and no drinking of water or any other liquid for about 26 hours, starting at sundown.

I begin the fast with my whole family on the night of Kol Nidrei, without too much difficulty. The next morning I walk to synagogue with my father and my uncle Simcha, who gives me a bar of my favourite Côte-d'Or Belgian chocolate to put in my sports jacket pocket in case I can't make it through the entire day.

The Gardens Synagogue, Cape Town

I spend part of the time in synagogue and part of the time with friends, roaming The Company Gardens around the synagogue. Every year, because the synagogue is near it, we make it a habit to go into the Cape Town art museum nearby. I have almost made it. Then, at 4 pm, a headache and hunger and thirst and weakness overwhelm me. I decide to take a bus home. And on the bus, I yield and open the chocolate bar and start to eat it.

One bite is enough to put an end to the integrity of my attempt. Either you have fasted or you have not. There is no going back. I eat the rest.

I like the Yom Kippur prayers in which you recite the sins of the past year. I like to mentally acknowledge the ones I can recall having committed.

AL CHEIT SHECHATANU

And for the sin which we have committed before You by hard-heartedness.

And for the sin which we have committed before You with an utterance of the lips.

For the sin which we have committed before You with immorality.

And for the sin which we have committed before You openly or secretly.

And for the sin which we have committed before You through speech.

And for the sin which we have committed before You by improper thoughts.

For the sin which we have committed before You by a gathering of lewdness.

For the sin which we have committed before You by impurity of speech.

And for the sin which we have committed before You by foolish talk.

For all these, God of pardon, pardon us, forgive us, atone for us.

For the sin which we have committed before You by false denial and lying.

And for the sin which we have committed before You by evil talk [about another].

For the sin which we have committed before You by the prattle of our lips.

And for the sin which we have committed before You by a glance of the eye.

For all these, God of pardon, pardon us, forgive us, atone for us. And for the sin which we have committed before You in passing judgment.

For the sin which we have committed before You by frivolity.

For the sin which we have committed before You by swearing in vain.

And for the sin which we have committed before You by a confused heart.

For all these, God of pardon, pardon us, forgive us, atone for us.

Chapter 19
Transformers

I live by my wits, I learn just enough to manage, like Hermes, the protector of travellers and thieves.

It is only at university that I discover that I am pretty good at physics and applied maths.

In my high school the science curriculum is very amateurish – mostly chemistry of some kind. No mechanics, no Kepler, no Newton. In maths, a fair amount of algebra, a ton of geometry, very little trigonometry. The only vaguely quantitative thing we learn is Boyle's Law. I never really try to learn, on my own, anything more advanced than what they teach us. I have the very strong unarticulated feeling, inculcated or inborn, that I need *to be taught* new stuff by someone senior *who knows it*. It never occurs to me that I can sit down and learn something new from a book, by myself. I must wait until I am at the right level to be taught it. This notion hampers me for years afterwards, and it is with difficulty that I overcome it, and only some of the time. I live by my wits, I learn just enough to manage, like *Hermes*, the protector of travellers and thieves.

First things first. I spend the post-matriculation summer of 1961/2 going to the beach at Clifton. Muizenberg is the family beach, though the Snake Pit provides social life and flirtations. But now that we are matriculated, Clifton is where the cool people go. From Oranjezicht my friends and I can walk uphill along the pipe track through the forest to the top of Kloof Nek and then down the other side to Clifton.

Walking down to Clifton from the Nek we often see off-duty city bus drivers in the woods with catapults and pebbles, shooting squirrels in the trees in order to make squirrel-tail furs for their wives[37] (or so we believe).

The Clifton beaches are numbered: First, Second, Third, and Fourth. Different ones become popular for different age groups in different years, the unspoken convention always shifting. Fourth is where Shulamit and her older friends go. My friends and I frequent First.

The Atlantic water feels icy, often 58°F or even lower, at least ten degrees colder than the sheltered False Bay water of Muizenberg. Your legs go numb with pain when you first enter the water in early summer, but then after a minute or two it becomes wonderful. We all try to get a suntan. By evening, going to a party, it's impossible to wear a shirt with a collar and tie over pork-rind shoulders and neck.

If you really want protection, you wear a shirt at the beach (not cool) or you smear yourself with white reflecting Nivea Cream (even less cool).

37 Yes, bus drivers in the Fifties were exclusively male.

This summer of 1961/2 I am getting ready for university. It is necessary, I have decided, to teach myself to touch-type because this is supposed to be important.

We have an old heavy mechanical typewriter at home, and I practice combinations from a manual I buy: *a, as, asd das, sad* ... over and over again until, after weeks, I can type any text containing capitals, lower case letters, and some punctuation marks at a reasonable pace. You need strong fingers to push down the mechanical keys that cause the typebars to hit the platen and paper, and you need an unnaturally strong little finger to push down the shift key. I give up practising around the time I should be learning the colons, semicolons, and numbers, so that in the end I can never type mathematics without looking at the keyboard.

In South Africa, as in Britain but in contradistinction to the United States, all undergraduate degrees are specialised. Before going to university, you decide on your field and then study only that area: B.Sc for science, B.A. for arts, B.Com for commerce. If you want to be a doctor, you go straight to medical school for six years, and one year after high school you are dissecting corpses and examining the insides of live bodies, some of them female. There's no premed.

I like literature and poetry but ... you have to specialise, and you can't afford to dawdle in this system, not only for economic reasons but also because you have the feeling that life is racing by and losing a year or two will set you back.[38] So, in my first year at UCT I take the standard four courses for pure science majors: Physics, Pure Maths, Applied Maths, and Chemistry. Each course runs a full year, with no electives. It's that simple.

In my high school matriculation exams I did just OK – A's for Science and Maths, B's for English, Latin, and Hebrew, **D for Afrikaans**.[39] For five years I have taken four languages – compulsory English and Afrikaans because the country is bilingual, Hebrew because I'm in a Jewish school, and Latin because I'm led to believe

---

38 Gap years (no such term exists) are for those whose parents think they need more maturity to handle university.

39 That wasn't as mediocre as it sounds; universal grade inflation came later.

that's what literate people do. But now at varsity I'm suddenly more in my element. I have a talent for Applied Maths and for the theory of Physics, I'm good at Pure Maths. In class you sit and take notes as fast as you can while the lecturer writes on the blackboard. Later you clean them up and fill them in as you work through the parts you couldn't get.[40] I learn everything assiduously, practice rederiving all the theorems and proofs over and over again at home, committing them to understanding, and then to memory by repetition.

I'm truly no good at physics experiments, and not good at Chemistry. Chemistry labs are a mystery to me – they give you some substance to analyse, and I don't have a clue. I never get to organic chemistry.[41]

The engineering students take the same Applied Maths and Physics courses as the pure science students do, but we regard them as animals, right-wing and rowdy in liberal mostly white University of Cape Town. They throw paper airplanes in class, revel in being uncontrollable. One of them, Chris, the son of the famous owner of a big firm of engineers, is arrested one night for urinating on The Grand Parade, the main public square in the centre of Cape Town. We look down on them; some of them study physics without ever learning calculus!

It takes me many decades before I realise how miraculous it is that people can use science and technology to put together something that actually works reliably. Now, bridges, airplanes, fruit blenders, shoes, what have you, confound me with admiration. I know a lot of theory, but I can't build anything reliably.

---

40 I still think this is a better way to learn than to be shown PDFs on a screen.

41 Chemistry still kind of mystifies me. I never properly understood pH and its importance in any deep way.

Chapter 20
Epiphanies

When my friends and I read Atlas Shrugged, *we think it's a subversively leftwing book.*

SIZE MATTERS

When I enter UCT in late February 1962 I am 5′ 4″. By November I am 5′ 11″ and have actual stretch marks. I'm not used to the idea of my new size. Towards the end of this first year, when I am standing with a crowd in the Maths Department corridor waiting for a tutorial to begin, Professor Skewes – who discovered one of the largest naturally occurring numbers in mathematics – asks one of the students to point me out. I hear the reply: *He's that tall fellow over there,* giving me a sudden burst of cognitive dissonance.[42]

THE BEAUTY OF CIGARETTES

At lunchtime at UCT we go to the Student Union to eat steak-and-kidney pies or Cornish pasties with chips – *England Expects,* even though we are no longer part of the British Commonwealth. We sit six to a table for a couple of hours and talk and talk and talk, and smoke.

It's great being able to smoke freely. I've been yearning for cigarettes for years, and now I can smoke without much embarrassment. I'm uncomfortable pulling out a pack in the Union and lighting up, because I look so young. But I do so anyhow.

A marvellously tempting plethora of foreign cigarettes is available at tobacconists in town. Sometimes I buy packs of Players, or Mills in tins, or other exotic English cigarette brands that I convince myself taste better than the regular South African brands

42 I am a human palimpsest with the stretch marks of 1962 still faintly visible.

– Rothmans, Ransom, Peter Stuyvesant, Viceroy. The packaging of the English brands is so beautiful and classy. I temporarily convince myself that though I will spend more money on them, I will smoke fewer of those cigarettes because they are so much better. My friend Philip claims smoking helps your hay fever.

UNNATURAL SOUTH AFRICAN LIFE

Before varsity, my interactions with Black people have always been based on differences in power. An embarrassing example: After I learn to drive and have a car of my own, I stop at the garage to get petrol and have my oil, water, and tires checked. One of the several Black attendants comes forward without speaking to do all this while I wait. I go to pay for the petrol at the kiosk inside. When I come out I give the shilling tip to the wrong man.

Being at UCT is an eye-opener. The university is mostly white[43], but anti-apartheid politics is everywhere. NUSAS, to which UCT belongs, is a liberal association of students at the English-speaking universities. Heads of the student council at UCT often subsequently become heads of NUSAS, and often subsequently get banned by the government. Sometimes they have their passports withdrawn and are forced to leave the country on an exit permit.

There are numbers of Coloured students and smaller numbers of Chinese, who are not considered white. Japanese, though, are *honorary whites* because Japan has reputedly purchased tons of pig iron from us. Nevertheless, many people have trouble distinguishing Japanese from Chinese.

There are few Blacks. One of them is Philip Kgosana who, after the massacre at Sharpeville in March 1960, led a peaceful march of 30,000 Blacks from Langa for miles along de Waal Drive past UCT into central Cape Town. They were protesting the South African pass laws.[44]

43 In 1957 there were fewer than 20 non-white students on a campus of approximately 5,000.

44 At this time I was in my last year in high school and everyone was terrified of what might happen when the marching crowd met the police. We were sent home early from school. My sister Shulamit worked in central Cape Town and my parents kept phoning her to find out if she was safe.

AVANT GARDE

Varsity, the student newspaper, is fabulous. The highlight is Anthony Eaton's humorous column each week.

It's the early sixties and there are *avant-garde* plays put on by student groups: Ionesco's *Rhinoceros,* Beckett's *Krapp's Last Tape,* Ann Jellicoe's *The Sport of My Mad Mother.* It's a different world, and a wonderful one.

ANTI-EPIPHANY

When my friends and I read *Atlas Shrugged,* we think it's a subversively leftwing book.

The South African political spectrum skews many degrees to the right. Books and people get banned. There is no TV (for if there were all the material would be from England or America, in English, too liberal for the pro-apartheid Nationalist Party). The degree of the country's rightward shift and attitudinal distortion is what makes us fail to grasp that *Atlas Shrugged* is not a leftwing book. The libertarian individualism of the novel's characters reminds us of the South African Liberal Party which seeks political rights for everyone independent of colour. Their slogan is "One man, one vote," which sounds vaguely Randian.

LIBERAL

When I am at UCT, "liberal" is a very good word.

One day one of the liberal politicians rebukes the avowedly "conservative" Nationalist pro-apartheid government that has increasingly instituted arbitrary detention laws:

> *You call yourselves conservative but we are the actual conservatives, preserving the democratic customs of the past. It's you that are the radicals.*

HOW TO LEARN BY MYSELF

I have always waited to be *taught* advanced stuff, but then, at UCT, I finally manage to learn some entire new fields by myself.

The first is in the summer after the end of my first year, when the Pure Maths Department instructs us to read a short book on *Functions of a Complex Variable* in preparation for the next year. I have never learned an entirely new topic by myself before, and over the course of several weeks I begin to master analytic functions and contour integrals.

The second is in my fourth year, when I am doing an Honours in Applied Maths. I write a mini-thesis on Unified Field Theories which try to combine Einstein's theory of general relativity with Maxwell's theory of the electromagnetic field. I learn tensor calculus and differential geometry. I search the literature in the library and manage to understand Einstein's attempts, Schrödinger's papers, and the Kaluza-Klein five-dimensional theory, and write up my thesis.

I am amazed then (and continue to be) that I can learn something untutored. It doesn't come naturally.

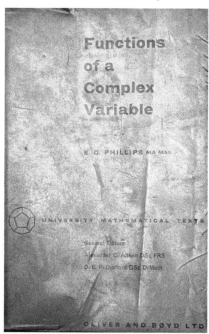

Chapter 21
Time's Fool

She leans forwards to touch someone's arm to accentuate something she says in conversation.

I don't really need money when I'm seventeen – my parents support me with no problem – but I decide to take a summer job at the end of my first year at university.

Through UCT's office I find out about a summer job at Jaggers, a wholesale department store in St George's Street that sells to other businesses. I interview for the position and am hired. Jaggers is famous and time-honoured among Jewish families: individuals get to shop wholesale there if they can claim a link through some friend's or family's business. My mother has taken me there many times to buy things through our cousins' Queens Hotel account. She bought me my first fountain pen there when I was in Standard 5, the first year we were allowed to abandon dipping pens and inkwells. It was a beautiful marbled blue Conway Stewart with a medium nib and cost £5.

If you buy something at Jaggers on one of the five or six higher floors, you can't simply pay and walk away with it. Instead, after you make your selection, a clerk charges the item to the wholesale account you are using and then sends it down a spiral chute to the basement where it is stored by customer name in bins labelled alphabetically. My job this summer is in the basement, where I collect items that come down the chute and put them in the correct bin. Then, when the customer comes to collect their purchase, I retrieve it and wrap it in brown paper.

CAPE TOWN, CAPE PROVINCE.
Wholesale importers (selling also from samples) :
John Garlick, 18–20 Adderley St.
Eaton Robins & Co., 74–76 Burg St.
Fraser & Co., 4 Burg St.
Stuttaford & Co., 62–70 Adderley St.
Cleghorn & Harris (Ltd.), Adderley St.
Fletcher & Co., 4 Darling St.
Brown, Lawrence & Co., 76–86 Barrack St.
Wm. Spilhaus & Co., 58 Strand St.
J. W. Jagger & Co., St. Georges St.
H. Jasper, Smith & Co., Trafalgar Place.

From a 1915 U.S. Dept of Commerce Report

I earn £8 a week. Working at Jaggers is a bit of a pose for me. I have taken the job in part because summer work is what self-respect and respect from other students at varsity requires. It's a real job, if only for six weeks until Christmas. I work from 8:30 until 5:00 on weekdays and then 8:30 to 1:00 on Saturdays.

I don't mix with many people there. There is one boy I know from high school, a couple of years older than me. There is a Sephardic woman in charge of the customer receipts, about 35 or even a bit older. She is a recent arrival, having fled the upheavals in the Belgian Congo. Manning the chute and the bins with me is Tokkie, who is Coloured and about my age, but already able to fend for himself. Tokkie is experienced, is a source of condoms for the white boys – he isn't afraid to ask for them at the chemist, and he resells them at a small profit to his clientele.

Tokkie is a much better parcel wrapper than I am, and tries to teach me. They don't give you Scotch tape. You have to fold brown paper around the item, hold the pointed folded edges in position and get a length of string from the roll to lie over it longitudinally, then make the two ends meet and cross and turn at right angles so they can wrap around the parcel latitudinally, and finally, when you get back to the starting point, tie a firm knot. Tokkie can manage all this with his hands and chin and teeth and produce perfect rectangular parcels. Mine always come out crooked and unprofessional.

It isn't easy.

Our day is broken by interludes. First, mid-morning tea break brought around on a wagon. Sometimes I chat for five minutes with the Sephardic woman, Mrs Azoulay, and listen to her French accent. She tells me she grew up on Rhodos in the Mediterranean and that later her family moved to the Congo. Then later, lunch. Sometimes I sit at the counter at the OK Bazaars' Wimpy's and buy a hamburger or hot dog and chips for one shilling and sixpence. Then I sit in the Gardens alone and smoke a cigarette. Later there's another mid-afternoon fifteen-minute tea break. The one relief from monotony is when the parents of someone I know come in to buy something and I retrieve and wrap the parcel for them.

That navy car could be my mother's 1948 Chevrolet.

At the Jaggers Christmas party at 4 pm one Friday we have music and refreshments. I dance a bit with some of the Afrikaner girls working there. At some point I ask Mrs Azoulay to dance, and she accepts. We dance very formally even though the music is mostly pop and rock and roll. We foxtrot to Frank Sinatra, her arm on my shoulder, mine around her back. She's a lot shorter than me, curved and full in the way girls aren't, has pretty, even teeth. She shows her gums slightly when she smiles.

One day the following week I leave Jaggers at 5 pm and decide to walk home. I head up St George's Street towards the Gardens and there in front of me is Mrs Azoulay going in the same direction. We say hello and discover we are both taking the path through the Gardens that leads to the suburbs on the slopes of the mountain. We talk animatedly, comfortably. She tells me about Rhodos and I tell her about university. It's a very very hot December day.

After walking uphill for about 15 minutes, she stops and says that this is the side road where she lives.

"It's very warm," she says. "We walked a long way. Would you perhaps like to have a quick cool drink before you continue?" She smiles in what seems to me a girlish almost shy way, and looks up at me.

We go in to the upper part of the house where she apparently lives alone. I sit down and she brings me a cool drink and then some sliced fruit. She tells me a bit more about her family's link to Rhodos. She excuses herself and says she has to change, and returns in a different dress and says it's new and turns to show it to me and asks if I like it. She says she will help herself to a bit of cognac and offers me a small glass too. She wipes her brow. She apologises for feeling a bit dizzy, says maybe it's the heat. I help her sit down on the couch where she leans back and looks up and sips from her glass. I sit next to her. Her eyes seem to blur.

I say I have to be home for dinner soon.

The next morning at tea-time I ask if she's feeling better. She's fine now, it was the heat.

I wonder why she lives alone. I watch her at work. She's subtler than the South African girls I know. She leans forwards to touch someone's arm to accentuate something she says in conversation. I imagine what people will say about someone twice my age.

I have one week more at work. We don't walk home together again.

Chapter 22
This Sporting Life

The unarticulated rule: if you kiss someone, you have to marry them.

There isn't much dating in my co-ed high school. Boys and girls pair up if they like each other, but it doesn't happen very often.

Now I'm at university, 16 or 17 or 18, and things are different.

Some boys still maintain the same pattern, asking a girl out if they like her. Others date for sport, going out with many girls in parallel and seeing what works for them. Some aim for sexual experience. I know a few who claim it's good to date nurses who work at Groote Schuur Hospital – their implicit assumption being that, since nurses' daily work is all about human bodies, they will have less inhibition about the whole business. And some try to optimise for the long run, dating marriageable girls on Saturday nights and girls they believe are more available on weeknights.

I'm in the ask-someone-out-only-if-you-like-them-a-lot category, and it's not often I like someone a lot. Absent that, I occasionally ask a girl out to a film just for the sake of going out.

 It's a formal business with lots of customs. You ask someone if they'd like to go to a film on a Saturday night. You buy tickets (all cinemas have reserved seats that must be booked in advance). You pick them up at their house and meet their parents. You drive to the bioscope. At intermission you go out to the foyer to buy a small box of fancy chocolates (Black Magic is the classiest) to give them to nibble on during the main feature. They offer you

some too. After the show you drive them home and drop them off. The film is the best part of it.

And every now and then girls ask you out. If they're in high school it's to their annual school dance, their hair pinned up in place and you in a white shirt and tie. If they are at university, it's to some wedding where they need a date. Or, on hot summer Christmas Eves, to a party that one of their friends is throwing. It's not much fun being the date of someone you don't especially like. Neither one of you knows exactly what's expected.

As for the girls I *am* attracted to, I'm a bit tentative about asking them out. We have exactly one telephone in our house; if I want to make a private call I have to unplug it from the jack in the hall, take it upstairs to my parents' bedroom where there is the only other jack, make the call, and then return it to the hall. Adding to the inhibition, I have been led to believe in the unarticulated rule: *If you kiss someone, you have to marry them.* No one actually proclaims that law in our house; it's ineffable, like God's name, and it doesn't need stating.

I manage to violate it, but it doesn't come easy. I would prefer to know that the girl likes me before I ask her out. So, often I ob-

sess about symbols: What did that remark of hers mean? Did I say
something inappropriate that I must now regret and try to correct?
And when I correct it will I make a new mistake? I am prone to this
kind of thinking – it's my specialty – analysing the deep metaphys-
ical meaning of social responses.

Part of a poem I publish in a university magazine:

Attempt at casual manner;
fly a tentative flag;
wave a contactual banner
parading feeling.
Yet you, either sensing dis-ease
or else inherently so
refuse to go along.

After too many of these episodes I decide on a new policy: If you
like someone, ask them out no matter what you think they might
think. Better to let them see how you feel, or even to declare it.
There's no shame in being attracted to someone. It will be much
worse, for someone like me, to think about what you should have
done than to simply be rejected.

Still, it's too complicated. Sometimes I think of Mrs Azoulay and
her womanly ways, who invited me in for a cool drink and, quickly
and unbidden, tried on her new dress for my approval. She was in
a different category from the girls I am trying to figure out how to
deal with.

One late afternoon, hanging around together in the street, some
friends and I discuss what age we'd choose if we had to remain
there forever. I suddenly think of a paragraph in Robert Musil's
Young Törless:

"He looked through the little windows and the crooked, narrow
doorways into the interior of the cottages with a gaze burning
so hotly that there was all the time something like a delicate
mesh dancing before his eyes ... here and there as some woman

bent over her work her skirt swung high revealing the hollows at the backs of her knees, or the bulge of a heavy breast showed as the linen tightened over it ... the cottages exuded a heavy sluggish air, which Törless eagerly breathed in."

To my friends' mystification I choose age 40. I fantasise that being 40 would make me just right for a life of passionate and yet domestic sexuality with Mrs Azoulay.

Chapter 23
The Cult and I
"Give me a girl at an impressionable age and she is mine for life."

When I am 15 I am sent to take extra Afrikaans lessons after school. My friend Don and I are to be coached by Mrs van der Merwe, a fortyish Afrikaner teacher who lives in nearby Tamboers Kloof. My mother drives us there and comes back to pick us up an hour later.

Mrs v. d. Merwe lives alone, seems a little lonely. We never see or hear of a Mr v. d. Merwe. During our first lesson I notice that, on the shelf in the dining room where we sit at the table, she has a strange electrical device attached by wires to what look like two small tin cans.

I'm curious and ask about it. She explains that she is studying scientology and that the device, an E-meter, can measure your feelings. She lets me hold the two tin cans, one in each hand, and tells me to think of something scary. The needle moves up. Then she tells me to think of something peaceful. The needle moves down. She explains how, by using this device, you can eventually become *clear*, untainted by harmful emotions and free of their consequences. *Halevai!*

Between the ages of 17 and 21 I too am a member of a (well-intentioned but unintrospectively powerful) sort of cult: the *Shomrim* (The Guards in Hebrew), the most senior age group of *Habonim* (The Builders), the Jewish aspirationally Zionist and Socialist-inspired youth movement I've mentioned many times earlier. We call it "the movement".[45] On Sunday mornings, as a *Madrich*, a group leader, I wear a derivative boy-scout uniform consisting of short khaki pants, a khaki shirt, long khaki socks, and a scarf folded into a triangle, rolled up and decoratively tied around the neck and held in place by a braided leather *woggle* – an atavistic Boer War uniform we still wear in the early 1960s.

Some *Habonim* Madrichim (Group Leaders)

My involvement in the movement starts as a child participant. From age eight to twelve I belong to *Hashtilim* (The Saplings). There are *Shtilim* groups in many of the suburbs. My group in Oranjezicht, named *Tel Yosef* after Joseph Trumpeldor, a Russian-born Zionist hero of the 1920s, meets every Sunday morning at The Orphanage. Under the guidance of our *Madrich* we learn Jewish history, play games, have competitions with other groups throughout Cape Town, and attend a national summer camp with members from all over the country. The structure is much like Lord Baden-Powell's colonial Boy Scouts, with the Mowgli mythology replaced by an evangelical pioneering *Aliyah* symbolism. *Hashtilim*'s logo is a brick

45 Those words "the movement" – as though there were only one in the universe – even now trip off my tongue like the verses of a poem learned by heart.

triangle containing a palm tree. Who on earth carefully made up the structure and the symbols we used? I don't know.

My sister Ruth is a *Madricha*, and when I am eight she takes me with her to a large several-weeks-long national summer camp at Ceres on the banks of the Breede River. I am allowed to go because she is there to keep an eye on me. It's fun. Every night there is a group campfire, and I become nearly famous for repeatedly entertaining people by singing *Thumbelina* from the Danny Kaye film about Hans Christian Andersen. In my opinion I give a great performance, shamelessly singing the words and miming the corresponding actions. Years later throughout high school some people who were at that camp will say "Thumbelina" when they see me.

At age 12 I graduate to the next group, *Bonim* (Builders), where there is a solid accent on acquiring expertise in classic Boy-Scout British-Empire skills: tying knots, pitching tents, making fires with one match, building camp furniture out of felled saplings lashed together with string, signalling with semaphore flags and with Morse code. You can use your scarf to make a tourniquet or a sling for a broken arm. We learn Jewish songs and Jewish history and 1958 Israeli geography, and pass tests and earn badges. I remember being coached by Selwyn Selikowitz,[46] fifteen years old to my thirteen, who later becomes a Cape High Court Judge in Cape Town. We attend sleep-away outdoor camps for three weeks in the summer, drink cocoa heated in a cauldron, and of course sing around the campfire. We spend ten days at "seminars" in old up-country hotels in the winter, a kind of indoor camping. All of this is overlaid with a back-to-nature romanticism reminiscent of the German *Wandervogel* movement of the early 20th century.

After that, at age sixteen or seventeen, if you haven't succumbed to the obligations of university, the sense that you should challenge

---

46 Welsh first name, East European last name. As my mother once perceptively pointed out about "Selikowitz," if you ever meet someone with a Polish last name and a Welsh, Irish, or Scottish first name, they will be Jewish and come from Southern Africa. Unlike the US, in South Africa immigrants from Eastern Europe or Russia often kept their last name but gave their kids Anglicised first names. Sometimes the parents – and even more so the grandparents – had a hard time pronouncing them correctly.

apartheid, and the attractions of serial dating, you become a member of the highest age group, *Shomrim*. That's the route I take. There are several thousand or more movement members countrywide in those three age groups, all impressively coordinated entirely by *Shomrim* youngsters in their late adolescent teens. They organise the business side of it, coordinate weekly subgroup meetings in each suburb, plan winter and summer camps, arrange educational trips to Israel to work on kibbutzim, hold annual youth congresses, and so on. There is virtually no adult help.

A few of the more idealistic members spend a year or two working full-time for the movement, on a small salary, in the downtown office. "I'm going to Office," someone might remark to you when they go in to do some movement work, as though there were only one office in the entire universe. Office is also a good place to socialise. We type bulletins and manifestos and educational material on wax stencils. We make movement songbooks. We create our own literary magazines. We reproduce them all on rotary Gestetner machines. The songbooks are heavy on spirituals but also contain other songs for campfire or bus-ride entertainment. Some are pretty amusing:

(Sung to the tune of *Song of the Volga Boatmen*)

My brother Joe and I
We went to school in Omsk
There we spent our time manufacturing atom bomsk
All the best atom bomsk comesk fromsk Omsk
Tomsk makes atom bomsk
But the be-e-e-st atom bomsk comesk fromsk Omsk.

My brother Joe and I
We went to school in Minsk
There we spent our time manufacturing safety pinsk
All the best safety pinsk comesk fromsk Minsk
Pinsk makes safety pinsk
But the be-e-e-st safety pinsk comesk fromsk Minsk.

My brother Joe and I
We went to school in Dniepropetrovsk ...

Many of us who still belong to the movement once we go to university are (mild) social misfits, uncertain or fearful about how to embark on an unsheltered life. We find succour in the weekly meetings and activities of the movement. Then, around 1964, when I am eighteen-and-a-half, my contemporaries who lead *Habonim* begin to pressure me and other members either to make a written commitment to emigrate to Israel, or to leave the movement.

By the end of high school I am drifting out of the movement. Nevertheless, on Friday nights I still attend meetings of our *Shomrim* group of teenagers age 16 and up, run by a member a few years older. We have serious and stimulating discussions about books and politics. Once, I give a lecture on the novels of C. P. Snow, author of the series *Strangers and Brothers*. I like Snow's approach to *The Two Cultures*, his idea that one should be familiar with both science and the arts. I especially like his dispassionate and yet compassionate view of the troubled relationships in his novels. But I don't have the personality for being a part of movements and group sing-a-longs and folk dancing – it all embarrasses me as I try to do it. I feel awkward and unconvincing – and yet here I am.

Meanwhile it is the early 1960s. After Friday night meetings we go to The Troubadour in Hope Street, to drink and listen to folk music. The performers sing spirituals, Dylan songs are coming into vogue, and Hoyt Axton's *Greenback Dollar* is a favourite. I think about how to get a new social life away from the movement. I date a bit. And then, in 1962 at the end of my first year at university, Justin Passwell, a medical student a couple of years older than me whom I both know and like from the Jewish school I attended, invites me to be a *Madrich* for eight-to-twelve-year-old *Shtilim* at the annual *Habonim* three-week summer camp by the sea at Onrus, seventy miles from Cape Town. I accept. And so I spend the first half of the summer working and earning money at Jaggers, and entire weekends meeting with other *Madrichim* to prepare for camp.

From Saturday afternoon to Sunday night a bunch of us, boys and girls (men and women?), camp out in Hout Bay, cook on a fire, prepare a syllabus of activities for the forthcoming camp, and learn commando-like outdoor activities from an Israeli ex-soldier. We learn how to commando-crawl around on beach in the dark, bodies pressed flat to the ground, propelling ourselves forward one foot at a time, trying not to be seen. *"Don't sit near your fire at night, that way the enemy can see you. Sit farther away in the dark, and then you can see them by the firelight when they approach."* We all bond and begin to meet during the week for fun as well as training. I'm friendly with Darylle, an independent girl from Stellenbosch who is just beginning to get involved in the movement.

Me peeling potatoes (in my white *Kova Tembel*) with other *Madrichim* and kids in the camp kitchen.

Finally, the three-week camp starts. We look after young boys and girls from all over the country, cook for them, put on entertainment at night around the campfire. Each of us sleeps in a tent on the ground with the five or six kids we're in charge of. When the kids are asleep we hang out on the beach late at night with the other *Madrichim*, flirting and smoking. The camp latrines are deep holes in the ground, covered by wooden planks with several holes carved in them, periodically topped up with quicklime. Flies buzz. I run a science group for the kids, telling them about the history of the universe, making hydrogen balloons from granulated zinc and hydrochloric acid.[47] We launch the balloons aloft with little

---

47 You could easily buy chemicals in a pharmacy in those days when pharmacists compounded most of their own prescriptions.

handwritten messages and watch them rise and float away, hoping someone will find the message when the balloons finally burst or deflate and drop back to earth.

It's a wonderful period. I am so busy *there is no time at all* to worry about personal problems.[48] I go to bed in the tent exhausted. The work is social, unlike the solitary labor of studying physics, banging your head against a book repeatedly. I love it and I love looking after young kids. And so, I'm hooked.

At the end of the summer Justin persuades me to become a regular year-round *Shtilim Madrich* and manage a group at the Orphanage in Oranjezicht. For the next three years I run a variety of groups, young kids on Sunday mornings or teenagers on Sunday nights, playing games and teaching them.

A year later I spend my summer vacation on a communal tour of Israel for South African *Habonim* youth. For six weeks we travel together, listen to lectures on Jewish history, work on a kibbutz, see the whole country at a time when luxuries are scarce. Coca Cola is unobtainable (the company fears an Arab boycott). Tel Aviv has only one restaurant, California, that sells hamburgers. The yolks of Israeli eggs are so pale that you wonder what they have done to the chickens. Like most everyone in the group I buy a *kefiyeh*, the Palestinian head-dress that is now a fashionable urban scarf in the movement. The irony is unapparent to me. Some of my friends, equipped with condoms by their parents for their first experience, visit prostitutes on Rechov Hayarkon or Ben Yehuda in Tel Aviv and come back to report.

I'm a person who takes other people's expectations too seriously. The increasing gung-ho-ness of the movement and its pressures begin to grate on me. I should laugh at it all but I can't.

There are the *Wandervogel-ish* slogans and principles that originated in the 1930s. One of the more memorable ones: A *member of Habonim is close to nature and simple in his ways. Habonim* has its own Hebrew pioneer words for everything official and ideological.

48 One of the great advantages and subliminal attractions of movements.

The movement's motto is *Aleh U'vneh* – go up and build – and the appropriate response is *Aloh Na'aleh* – we will indeed go up. The first line of the movement's archaic-sounding song is *"Habonim, strong builders, we lads have become,"* the lads being a nice Scottish-Jewish touch. Somewhere in the song is a couplet that goes, "We pause not for laggards but build, brick by brick, A mighty foundation with shovel and pick." Some of us invariably sing the last phrase as "shovel and prick."

There is an unwritten prejudice against girls wearing makeup. We are supposed to sanctimoniously look down on bourgeois social life and its ambitions. The highest aspiration is to upend the traditionally 19th century Jewish social structure of labor, which, we are taught, was an unfortunately inverted triangle, its top disproportionately heavy with professionals and brainworkers and its bottom too light with the agricultural and manual labourers that should have provided a stable societal base. There should be more workers and fewer *luftmenschen*. Labor is noble. The best thing you can do is emigrate to Israel, live on a kibbutz, and earn your keep by manual labor in a communal setting. On some kibbutzim the children are brought up communally, sleeping in a children's unit apart from their parents. Some young men of my generation in South African *Habonim* choose to become fitters and turners or plumbers rather than go to university. For several years the movement runs a *Hachsharah* (preparation camp), a communal kibbutz-style farm within South Africa where you can live and learn agricultural skills to prepare for kibbutz life.

Since entering university, my social life has revolved largely around *Habonim*. The years flow by. Weekends involve Friday night discussions among contemporaries, Saturday night get-togethers with our own entertainment and skits, Sunday mornings or evenings running a weekly meeting for a group of kids. Late at night we drive to The Harlequin or The Doll's House drive-in restaurants for toasted cheeses, chips, and milkshakes. We sit in our car until late at night talking about intellectual stuff, morality, and girls. It's fun.

For me, this cloistered and romantic haven comes to a crisis during my final years at university. Now, around 1964, the 19- and 20-year olds who run the movement start nudging us harder and harder to fulfil its aims. They institute an *Aliyah Register*, an oath you have to sign in order to continue to be a member of the movement. Your signature will certify that you intend to fulfil *Chalutzik Aliyah* (a pioneering emigration to Israel), or, failing that, at least some kind of bourgeois *Aliyah*. If you won't sign, the charismatic senior members – most vocally my friend Darren, who himself later went to and then left kibbutz after a few years – scorn and even shame you.

But I know I most likely will not emigrate to Israel. And I won't give up physics in order to live on a kibbutz. I wouldn't live on a kibbutz even if I did give up physics.

GIVE ME A GIRL AT AN IMPRESSIONABLE AGE AND SHE IS MINE FOR LIFE.

So, though I still enjoy working at camps in the summer, somewhere around the age of twenty I cut loose from the movement and its constraints, feeling a little bitter at the hole in my social life that follows. It doesn't matter as much as I fear because I leave for New York a year later.

But the movement left its deep and unfaded marks on me, many of them good. Otherwise I wouldn't be writing about it.

I didn't object to the love of Israel, and I never then or now doubt our need for it. We were barely a post-holocaust generation, ever mindful of where we came from and what we lost. What bothered me was the self-righteous, I-know-what-you-should-do attitude of people who pressured me. Years later, few of them remained in Israel, and an even smaller number still lived on kibbutz. I should have smiled at their internal contradictions.

Chapter 24
Some Bits About My Character

The past is always present.

It gets formed very early, and doesn't change much. I'm the same person always.

I get attached to people very quickly, and it lasts a long time, perhaps forever.

I don't like letting go of things. I don't like parting, from anyone.[49]

I don't like showing people that they have hurt me. I pretend to them that they haven't.

I remember injustices, and resent them for a long time.

*

I'm not very professional. I learn the least amount I need in order to manage, even in research. I'd rather try to figure out how to do something myself than learn how to do it. This can be counterproductive.

I like to understand what there is to understand by using what I already know.

There are some books and subfields I've been intending to study my whole life, but I can never get down to them.

49 Parting is a sort of rejection. I don't even like hanging up the phone.

I imagine that anything I don't know isn't worth knowing.

I foolishly imagine I can be good at anything if I try.

I'm slow and perhaps, occasionally if I'm lucky, slightly deep rather than quick.

I'm very persistent.

*

I don't like being in organisations. I wish I did.

I hate working for people and sometimes hate people I work for.

I like to work in small groups or by myself.

I need company and I need responses from people. I will sometimes say things I shouldn't in order to have an interaction.

I have an unfortunate "eagerness to impart unnecessary information." I disclose rather than hide my problems.

*

The past is always present.

I sometimes mope but I don't get depressed.

I complain a lot.

It took me a while to realise this, but ...

> *In all its phenomena the outer world is filled with divine splendour,*
> *but first we must have experienced the Divine within ourselves if*
> *we are to discover it in the surrounding world.* – Rudolf Steiner

Chapter 25
The Red and the Black

As the door opens I register flesh and solidity and a fullness that seems to burst all boundaries.

Odalisque couchée aux magnolias. Henri Matisse. (1923)

In my last year of high school I take painting-and-drawing lessons one afternoon a week at the Frank Joubert Art School in Claremont. Our teacher is a late-thirties refined-looking Dutch woman with brown rounded arms, a rounded full body, and long elegant legs. She is a new immigrant to South Africa, having fled the Dutch Indonesian ex-colonies after the troubles there, and she has café-au-lait skin and a chalk-white smile. She is corporeal and good-natured, down-to-earth and solid. In fact, she could easily be mistaken for a Cape Coloured, whose skin shades cover a wide colour spectrum. Despite this, she is strongly pro the Nationalist apartheid government.

During class she likes to slip her small bare brown feet out of her brown moccasins and wiggle her toes on the floor beneath the table at the head of the studio. Once, looking down at her feet, she gives us a mock-serious lecture on the dangers of not drying them thoroughly after a bath, and proceeds to demonstrate, with words and in great detail, how to use an imaginary towel to carefully dry between her toes. The glimpsed nooks and crannies of her body seem more intriguing and mysterious than the bodies of the bland younger-than-me girls I've liked. Her easy way is something I've never seen.

Her husband occasionally comes to art-school functions too. He is a portly gruff sensual-looking man, dresses in dark suits like the men in Rembrandt's sombre group portraits of Amsterdam patriarchs. A year later we hear that he has left her and their late-teenage daughter for another woman.

The Syndics of the Clothmakers Guild. Rembrandt. (1662)

My uncle in Tel Aviv, a newsagent, regularly sends me copies of *Mad Magazine*, hard to find in South Africa. One of the issues has a spoof on vending machines, and one of the cartoons shows a large machine with women of various styles behind the glass doors, each door carrying a labelled button to push after you insert your quarter. One of the labels reads "Pleasantly Plump" and the woman in the cartoon behind the glass reminds me of the art teacher. The label evokes a world of frequently savoured familiar yet exciting passions.

In my third year at university I'm a *Habonim* counsellor in charge of a bunch of boys between eight and twelve years old who all live in Oranjezicht. We meet every week on Sunday morning in the Orphanage. Everyone is in standard khaki *Habonim* uniform. I administer corny Boy-Scout-style opening ceremonies in Hebrew, organise scavenger hunts, teach bits of Jewish history, play rounds of soccer or cricket, give quizzes, teach campcraft and other scouting-y things.

One Sunday a new eleven-year-old joins the group and soon becomes a regular. He has a charming open way about him. I feel paternal, and he has asked me for a book on physics so that he might learn something. I tell him I have one aimed at a layman audience and I will bring it to him, and so, one weekday afternoon, I drive over to his house, about five minutes from ours. I park in front, and take the book with me.

I push open the low front gate in the centre of the hip-high brick wall facing the street and walk down the stairs. The front door is a frame of translucent glass made-up of multiple small lenses, through each of which I can see a kaleidoscopic interior. I ring.

Something happens.

I hear footsteps and after each one the soft rhythmic flap of a loose shoe against a foot. I see the blurred shape of a pink housecoat approaching through the glass. As the door opens I register flesh and solidity and a fullness that seems to burst all boundaries.

She is in her late thirties. Her hair is dark black, thick and stiffly coiffed above a broad white forehead; she has heavy black carefully plucked eyebrows above dark brown eyes, a thick sensual nose, and somehow impatient red lips. I think momentarily of Myrtle, Tom Buchanan's energetic and common mistress in *The Great Gatsby*.

"I've brought a book for Daniel," I say.

"I'm Mrs Gold," she says. Her voice is deep and sonorous and slow, no-nonsense, but she smiles and looks me over. "Daniel told me about you. He's not here now, he'll be back soon, but come inside." She holds out her hand. Her nails are bright red, her arms ample and full below the short sleeves of the housecoat. Her palm feels big and warm.

She leads me into a plain comfortable living room. Her cork-soled mules (I don't know that that's what they are called until much later) tap up and down against her heels as she walks. The toes and backs are open, with just a strap across the arch. She seats herself in the armchair opposite me and leans back, crossing one leg over the other at the knee, dangling one shoe off the front of her raised right foot. Red toenails peek through the front; a white heel emerges smooth and round at the back. She is too ample to be graceful, but she isn't ungraceful either. I suddenly wonder about her carnal life.

The maid soon brings a small tray with a tea pot, two cups and saucers, milk and sugar and some home-made biscuits. Mrs Gold pours me a cup, and then pours one for herself. She takes a pack of cigarettes off the side table and taps one out and lights it and takes a quick draw.

"Oh my goodness, sorry, I should have asked," she says as an afterthought. "Do you smoke?"

"Sometimes, yes," I nod. "I wouldn't mind one."

"Of course," she smiles. She rises and walks towards me with the pack, taps it upside down on the coffee table to shake the cigarettes loose, and proffers the pack. I take one. She offers me her lighter, a small solid slim silver Ronson that looks too angular for her soft fingers. She reminds me of the art teacher, though there is no specific resemblance.

"What are you studying at university?" she asks. I explain about physics and particles and fields. We drink tea and smoke and talk about her son for ten minutes, like two adults. Then Daniel arrives and she fusses over him.

"It was nice talking," she says when I say I must go. "Drop in again if you're near."

After that I make my path often cross that of Mrs. Gold's. Sometimes, driving home from university or to neighbouring suburbs to visit friends, I see her white four-door tail-finned Chev parked in various places. It's a talisman. Sometimes it's in front of my friend's flat in Vredehoek where she takes her daughter for music lessons. Sometimes it's opposite another friend's house in Oranjezicht where she visits her sister-in-law. She seems to spend her days driving her two young children.

There is no visible husband. I learn that he owns a farm in the Karoo, hardly ever comes to Cape Town. The kids visit him there during vacations. Daniel tells me his father has to be at the farm. The strangeness of this arrangement never occurs to me.

When I drive to university I begin to take circuitous routes that run via her house. On rainy weekend days I take long walks in her neighbourhood, hoping for glimpses. If I see her car parked outside her house, then sometimes – not so often as to be too noticeable – I allow myself a visit, usually on the pretence of saying hello to her son.

Now when I knock on the door, I wait for approaching footsteps and the vague pink shape of the housecoat through the glass. Sometimes the maid answers the door, and, now familiar with me, gives a smile and then calls up the stairs, *Madam, your young man is here.*

For twenty or thirty minutes we sit in her living room. After the maid brings tea she offers one of her cigarettes and I inhale too as I watch her take long drags on the cork filter she places between her lips. She likes to talk, and, self-assured though she is, seems puzzled by young people's lives in the 1960s. She quizzes me on what I read, on politics, on what it's like to be young and at university. She wants to know what her son and daughter should learn about.

I think about her. I wonder what to do.

Over time Mrs Gold tells me about herself. She grew up in a small *dorp* north of Cape Town. Her husband had been brought to South Africa from Lithuania as a 14-year-old long before World War II. She was eighteen, fourteen years younger than him and just out of school at the end of the war when they married. They moved to a farm he bought in the Karoo. A few years after that, when her first child was born, she moved to Cape Town. Her husband kept running the farm.

Now her life is filled with looking after children, seeing relatives, being involved in charity events, raffles, and used-clothing drives.

"I married early, you know," Mrs Gold says to me one day between cigarettes. "Straight out of school. In the *bundu* you married and became a housewife. Nowadays girls need time to find themselves – they shouldn't compete to find a husband so soon."

"According to Schopenhauer," I reply stupidly, "all women are natural competitors. They're like plumbers or shoemakers, all in the same trade." I explain who Schopenhauer is.

She nods seriously and frowns a little, takes another drag on her cigarette.

"Maybe," she says slowly, " ... that could be. At least when they're young. I wonder if I was like that. It's a little sad, you know, how we set out in life with no idea of what will happen. Or the wrong idea. That hasn't happened to you yet, you're lucky ... I live differently now from what I expected."

I like her and I can see she likes me. I take what I can: the flattery of being taken seriously, the surreptitious glances at her incipiently vulnerable body, the beginning-to-get-heavy contours of her face, the full figure and legs, the slow curvaceous walk when she's relaxed, the index finger impatiently tapping on the cigarette to knock off ash, the sticky red imprint of her lips on the end of the cork filter, a glimpse of a slip between two buttons of the pink housecoat, the way she leans over to touch my arm, intimate and casual when she wants me to refocus my attention on some new question.

Her whole life seems bare of men, and yet ... she chooses her clothes and paints her nails to look attractive. Why would anyone do that if they weren't thinking about men?

One Sunday afternoon I go driving on a country road near the local quarry and see Mrs Gold and Daniel walking together on the sidewalk, accompanied by another mother and son. I slow down and wave to them as I drive by, but keep going. When I turn my head left and back to look at them and wave, the steering wheel turns left with me. The car rides up briefly on the empty country sidewalk and then comes down again. I hope they don't notice.

On a rainy weekday afternoon during university winter holidays I take a solitary walk through suburban streets to pass her house. The windows upstairs and down are all dark except for the kitchen. I open the gate and walk down to the front door and ring the bell.

She opens the door dressed in her housecoat. "Oh, no one's here, Daniel and Sandra have gone out of town to the farm for the week, and I gave the maid the afternoon off." She looks worn, not right. "Do you want to come in for a while?"

Tea and cigarettes. She looks distracted as we talk about politics, South Africa, Israel. Suddenly, between puffs, she covers her face and sobs for a moment. I am about to ask what is wrong when she waves her hand up and down in a negative ignore-it sign.

"Don't ask me anything, please," she says. She takes a tissue from the table and wipes her eyes.

I look at her. She's pale. No red lipstick. Her fullness and freshness are gone. I feel deep and sad for her, paternal, and filial too. Shakespeare jumps into my head.

Love's not Time's fool, though rosy lips and cheeks
Within his bending sickle's compass come;
Love alters not with his brief hours and weeks,
But bears it out even to the edge of doom.

I have been wanting to touch her for weeks. I walk over to her armchair and stand over her, lean down and stroke her black hair, kiss her forehead. She looks up confusedly.

"What *are* you *doing?*" she says sharply, and stands up quickly.

"It came over me," I say, and back off. "What could I do? I'm sorry you're sad."

A softer kinder look comes over her.

"My dear! It's alright! Don't be upset! I didn't expect *that*," she says.

She has cheered up and half chuckles. "Oh, so *romantic*," she says, with a touch of mockery. "You're from a different generation, I never really had those feelings. I didn't have time for relationships," she says in a continuing stream of statements. "I went straight from parents to husband to children."

She sits down again and smiles and says, "Sit, let's have some more tea and a cigarette."

She changes the subject. Later, when I feel I should leave, she walks me to the door.

"Please please don't be insulted," she says looking straight at me. "It's alright. I like talking to you. I'm sorry I'm upset today, I reacted too much."

She leans forward and kisses me lightly, right on the lips.

I return in my car the next day in the late afternoon. She looks a bit agitated when she opens the door.

"Is everything OK?" I ask.

"Thank you for being with me yesterday," she says. "I have troubles. I cannot talk about them ... I read my horoscope today and it said everything will be ok!"

"I'm sure it will," I say. "Things will work out."

"Do you really think so?" she asks me, leaning back, entwining her solid legs about each other shyly as though she were a child, looking up at me almost coquettishly.

"Yes I do."

"Really?"

"Yes. Bad things will pass. I know how it feels sometimes."

"I'm being silly, I'm sorry. How can you know?" She smiles. "But you're making me feel better anyway."

She makes tea.

"I've been having such a difficult time for months," she says quietly while we sip. "Thank you for helping me."

We talk.

When the time comes I prepare to go to my car. It's no longer light. She accompanies me outside, which she's never done before, and waits while I open the car door. She looks sad.

"I can keep you company for a while if you like. Shall I?" I ask.

"Yes," she says, slowly and softly, assenting with a grave nod, moving her face up and down through such a long vertical arc that, at its nadir, I can see the crown of her head.

I decide to tell the truth.

"I don't feel like leaving you anyhow," I say.

She moves forward in the dusk, tilts her head up, and puts her lips against mine. I'm much taller than her.

"Then don't," she says, and kisses my mouth and then my cheek.

My heart fills with all the kinds of love I know about. I see her yearning for something I cannot properly understand and I see that she sees my yearning. I kiss her cheek, and she kisses me back.

"Come back inside," she says with a sigh.

Chapter 26
Distant Drums
• Plotting resonances • Programming a computer to write poems
• The serendipity of acne • Mystic teachers

> *Dim drums throbbing, in the hills half heard,*
> *Where only on a nameless throne a crownless prince has stirred,*
> *Where, risen from a doubtful seat and half attainted stall,*
> *The last knight of Europe takes weapons from the wall,*
> *The last and lingering troubadour to whom the bird has sung,*
> *That once went singing southward when all the world was young,*
> *In that enormous silence, tiny and unafraid,*
> *Comes up along a winding road the noise of the Crusade.*
>   from *Lepanto* by G. K. Chesterton

Somewhere during my third year at UCT, while majoring in physics and applied maths, I begin to detect the sound of distant drums. There are universities in England and America where serious people go to do advanced physics. (Yes, we say "to do" physics, not "to study" physics. Physics is a vocation.) People I know have pulled up stakes and gone abroad to get a PhD, people serious and ambitious and willing to leave home even though they don't have to. They want to do something wonderful.

Some of them do. I first learn about overseas PhD-ers from my Oranjezicht neighbour Jeffrey Bub, the older brother of my classmate Julian. Jeffrey has left Cape Town to do a PhD in London with David Bohm on hidden variable theories of quantum mechanics, and will eventually become a well-known philosopher of quantum mechanics.

The Physics Department likes to tell you it's not necessary to leave UCT to do good physics. But, when we learn quantum mechanics, they teach it as though it's mysterious and hard to grasp, something bewildering they learned from a textbook.[50] You *can* get a PhD at UCT, but I know in my heart that Cape Town is not the place for fundamental physics. And that's what I care about.

At the end of my third year I'm about to graduate with a B.Sc. I take a summer job working for Professor Frank Brooks, a skilled nuclear experimentalist in the UCT Physics Department. He doesn't really need me. He is being kind, because first, he is kind, and second, I got the class medal for physics that year.

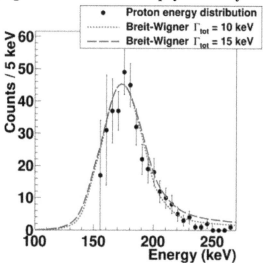

50 In 1966 quantum mechanics was barely 40 years old, less distant in the past from then than The Standard Model is from now. You were encouraged to simply master it, "Shut up and calculate!" as people very seriously joked. As I wrote in *My Life as a Quant* of my experience of Columbia in 1966: "Physics in the United States was much more professional, hard-nosed and business-like. Columbia's physics department, I saw over and over again, didn't think of modern physics as something esoterically advanced and difficult, to be revealed to you only when you crossed some threshold and finally became an initiate. They expected you simply to plunge right in." Today, 60 years later, physicists have come three-quarter circle. Though quantum mechanics is still their undeniably accurate tool, they admit that it is bewildering and not as routine as they pretended when I first came to Columbia. Steven Weinberg, one of the co-discovers of The Standard Model, wrote in 2017: "I'm not as sure as I once was about the future of quantum mechanics. It is a bad sign that those physicists today who are most comfortable with quantum mechanics do not agree with one another about what it all means." *Tempus fugit.*

Professor Brooks is studying resonances, the states of a nucleus that occur when you bombard it with high-energy charged particles that excite its insides by colliding with it. The resonances survive only a short time as entities and then decay into other particles and other nuclei. It's called a resonance because the nucleus, when hit with the appropriate energy, resonates like a child's swing being pushed at its natural frequency. He performs these experiments with graduate students at the Van de Graaff accelerator at Faure, a nearby suburb.

I am very unknowledgeable about all of this – I have pretty much done only *theoretical* physics and don't know much nuclear physics. He and his students have measured the number of decays per second of each metastable resonance they create as they vary the energy of the bombarding particle. My work for him involves merely plotting the number of decays as a function of the bombarding particle's energy. When you excite the nucleus into a short-lived metastable state by hitting it with something close to the right resonant energy, you observe a peak in the number of decays that's described by the Breit-Wigner formula.[51] The width of the peak measures the lifetime of the state, which can be compared with the prediction of nuclear theory.

My job is to use a pencil and a *French Curve* to draw smooth lines through the experimental data points, and then measure the width of the resonance. I'm not very good at this, and when Prof Brooks needs it done more precisely, one of his graduate students will probably do it.

I drive to university every day for six weeks in the summer. Each morning I settle at my bench in one of the physics labs to plot my graphs. In the room next door is Vic, already working on a Master's. He collects unused bags of donated human blood from nearby Groote Schuur Hospital, freeze-dries it, and then measures something (maybe radioactivity? I don't exactly know). When a spin-

---

51 Exciting the nucleus by varying the incoming energy of the bombarding particle is a bit like tuning your analog radio onto the right frequency of a radio station you want to listen to. It gets louder and clearer as you get closer to the broadcast frequency.

ning flask of blood has been totally freeze-dried, a giant bloody scab lines the inside of the flask. A disgusting cloud of vapour fills the room, enveloping everything, and working its way unremittingly into my clothes, which I have to wash as soon as I get home.

But then suddenly that summer, UCT acquires an ICT 1301, a mainframe computer made in England and lodged in the new computer centre. The language it understands is MAC – Manchester Auto Code. Prof. Brooks sends me to a week-long course on learning to program. He wants me to write a program to automate the plotting of the resonance curves as X's on a line printer, thereby producing a primitive kind of graphics that will eliminate the need for hand-drawing and measuring.

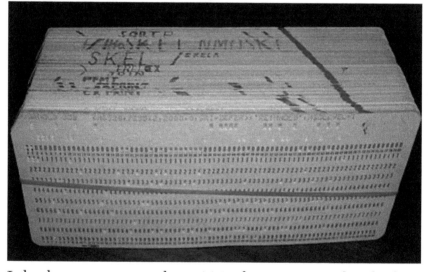

I develop my programs by writing them on paper, line by line, composing and revising them as though they are an essay. There are no such machines as terminals and editors. When you think your program is right, you punch it, instruction by instruction, as coded holes onto cards using a keyboard that controls a mechanical punch. To check for typos, you then put the cards into a very similar machine, a verifier, on whose keyboard you *type the same instructions again*. The verifier checks the match against each card. Then you submit it to the computer centre, where the operators run it at night. Most of the time it comes back with a typo that you have to fix, one you would have caught beforehand if you'd been more careful.

Some days I hang out with Dubbi, a nuclear physics student a couple of years ahead of me. Sometimes we go to The Pig and Whistle, a favourite pub of students, where a whole beer will leave me slightly woozy. I drive anyway.

One day I decide to surreptitiously use the computer to create multiple random poems. I code up hundreds of words as print statements, generate hoped-for random numbers by looking at the last digits of Sine(N) where N cycles one by one through the integers, and use the numbers to determine which print statement to execute and when to generate a line break.

I prime the print statements with melancholy romantic words, hoping to generate dreamily sad love poetry.[52]

At heart I'm a theorist. And, at the end of my third year, majoring in both physics and applied maths, I find that the rigour of the advanced mechanics and relativity taught in the Applied Maths

---

52 I didn't realise then that continuing to do that could be a serious endeavour rather than just fun.

Department is more to my taste than the sloppier maths of the Physics Department.

For South Africans, England is the natural place for post-graduate study. So, I have been applying to the DAMTP (Department of Applied Mathematics and Theoretical Physics) to do a PhD in Cambridge, and have been corresponding with Prof. J. C. Polkinghorne, a theoretical physicist who years later would become an Anglican priest.

Then, in 1965, while I am completing a one-year B.Sc. (Hons) in Applied Maths, I serendipitously stumble on a path that leads to studying in the U.S. It's all the consequence of a bad case of acne that sends me to a dermatologist.

The dermatologist is the uncle of David Dorfan, a Capetonian who is already doing a PhD in New York City at Columbia University in experimental particle physics under Leon Lederman. David is part of an experiment that discovers an antideuteron produced in high energy particle collisions. It's not really a surprise to find that antideuterons can be produced – everyone believes that the deuteron must have an antiparticle. Still, it's nice.

By coincidence, my sister Ruth, now a clinical psychologist, had helped David's younger brother Jonathan successfully overcome a junior-school diagnosis of "poor concentration" ten years earlier at the Child Guidance Clinic at UCT.[53] The Dorfan family is very grateful to her, and they and the dermatologist uncle now take a benevolent interest in me. They encourage me, like David, to apply for fellowships to study physics in the U. S. In particular, they recommend applying to the Institute for International Education (IIE) that shepherds your application to several schools simultaneously. I write essays about what I want out of life and academia, about how I want to discover the fundamental laws that drive the universe. I collect recommendations from university lecturers and high school teachers. Shulamit and Albie Sachs help me with my cover letter and application.

53 As you can see from the Wikipedia article about Jonathan Dorfan, my sister was successful. Jonathan eventually became an experimental particle physicist and subsequent head of SLAC, where, years later as a postdoc, I spent several summers doing theoretical particle physics.

I don't have a clue about what I'm embarking on – a life abroad away from everyone I know.[54] Automaton-like, at first with excitement and then with a growing fear I won't acknowledge, I push on.

If not for the acne, I might have remained in South Africa or gone to study in Cambridge.

At UCT I like the rigorous approach of the Applied Maths Department, and take tensor calculus, differential geometry, and general relativity from Professor J.H.M. Whiteman, a serious elderly man with very small crab-like handwriting. For my winter project I do a literature survey of unquantized *Unified Field Theories*, attempts to unify classical gravitation with classical electromagnetic theory. The only way to get books on the topic is to search the UCT library. To find papers I read through *Mathematical Abstracts* and track them down or order them from interlibrary loan. I read papers by Schrödinger, Einstein, Kaluza and Klein, Weyl, Eddington, ... all in their own different ways trying to extend general relativity and its metric tensor so that it can accommodate the *antisymmetric electromagnetic tensor field F* that satisfies Maxwell's equations. I learn all this by myself, fortified by visits to Professor Whiteman's home in Pinelands where we discuss what I've been reading. I am amazed at my temporary ability to work my way through many papers on things I have never been taught, to extract their essence without fear. I learn to skim and then plunge.

Whiteman is writing a book on Quantum Mechanics, a draft of which he sends to Dirac. He tells me that Dirac approves of it. We never discuss anything except physics and applied mathematics.

---

54 O Younger People! In the 1960s it was virtually impossible to call from Cape Town to New York and vice versa. There was no internet or email, only letter writing. The best you could do was to make a three-minute "trunk call" that had to be booked and scheduled in advance at great expense. When people travelled by air, they sent a telegram on arrival saying ARRIVED SAFELY. So difficult was communication that David Dorfan's father, who was a ham radio operator, persuaded David in New York City to seek out other amateur radio operators so that he could have brief audible radio contact with his family.

It's far easier to communicate with anyone anywhere in the world today than it was to communicate between New York City and Cape Town 60 years ago.

Many many years later I will discover that Whiteman is a man of interests and talents that he never mentions, from music to mathematics to mysticism. For 55 years he is the journal editor for the South African Society of Music Teachers. He is a *scientific* mystic, a phenomenologist perhaps. He often refers to the Vienna Circle and Husserl.

Whiteman aimed to establish mysticism as scientific – a field capable of being incorporated into science. His emphasis was on unobstructed observation, not on theorising about what he called 'the inner constitution of nature'. His mysticism aimed to provide an 'open-minded, rigorously tested, rationally coherent and illuminating' treatment of non-physical states and happenings.
(Excerpted from *The Psi Encyclopedia*)

I wish I had known that when we talked those many years ago.

Chapter 27.
1966 and All That...

How is it that I know myself so poorly?

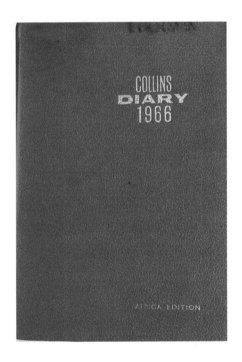

Nine hundred years after the Battle of Hastings, I begin to internalise the fact that I will soon leave South Africa. Shulamit and Albie encourage me to leave – Why? Don't they know that I will never ever return? – and help with my applications to the IIE in New York. I go down to the U.S. Consulate on Cape Town's foreshore for an interview with an American junior consul, Charlie, who is also an acting representative of the IIE. He tells me that he went to Columbia and that if I end up there I should go to Tom's Restaurant at 112th and Broadway and give his regards to Nick. Nine months later I do just that. The manager says they have no Nicks there, but when I insist, they bring up from the basement a dishwasher called Nikos. He does not know any Charlie.

Every Greek-owned restaurant probably has a Nick.

HOW IS IT THAT I KNOW MYSELF SO POORLY?

The IIE requires that applicants choose three American universities. I choose Columbia because it's in New York and because David Dorfan went there; I choose Caltech because Feynman had received the Nobel prize the previous year; I choose Berkeley because it sounds like the coolest place to be – there's the Free Speech Movement. All three have good physics departments.

Rationally, I grasp the reality that I will soon leave Cape Town. But my emotional intelligence goes into a hibernation that allows me to avoid thinking about the future in any detail. I suppress all thoughts of what it will be like to be 8,000 miles away from anyone I know. When my father, awkwardly but with good intentions, tries to broach the difficulty of my going far away from home alone and for good, I irritatedly cut him off.

I have been away from home many times before, on vacations with friends, on a tour to Israel, working in *Habonim* camps, but never all on my own without the ability to speak with (or get comfort from) anyone I know. It will affect me badly. But now in 1966 it's beyond my capacity to give any of this a thought.

The moment of my eventual arrival in a state of foreign isolation in August 1966 in far-away New York City will soon open a wound that never totally heals. Or perhaps it will reopen an unremembered wound inflicted much earlier.

When I was eight Ruth would read me Coleridge's *The Rime of the Ancient Mariner:*

Alone, alone, all, all alone,
Alone on a wide wide sea!
And never a saint took pity on
My soul in agony.

It wasn't quite that bad when I arrived in New York, but it was bad. Ever since then I've identified with lonely people.

Meanwhile, in March 1966, I am still in Cape Town and beginning a Master's degree with Prof. Whiteman. I am reading Dirac's _Principles of Quantum Mechanics_. This is the book that my _Habonim_ sociology-studying friend Darren mocks because he cannot imagine that any book can take more than a week to grasp.

I share an office at varsity with another Master's student, Mike Viljoen, who is working on modeling the weather with Prof D. G. Parkyn. Prof. Parkyn models the earth as a rotating cylinder rather than a rotating sphere because this simplification gets rid of a degree of freedom, thereby minimising the computing needed to solve the hydrodynamic equations. But the ICT 1301 still doesn't have enough speed. Mike and Prof. Parkyn need to gain every bit of efficiency if they want to run their programs fast. One of the operations they frequently perform is taking the square root of a number, a common and prosaic function in any programming language. The MAC language provides its own built-in function for square root, but that doesn't run fast enough for their needs. Prof. Parkyn makes Mike write his own square root algorithm in machine code.

Mike is very different from me. He's an Afrikaner living with his girlfriend. He's probably a Nationalist, and a boxer too. We get along well in our shared office and kid around all the time. Periodically we relax by sparring, with him teaching me a bit more about how to block his blows.

And so the year begins to pass. I go out with one or two girls, in series. I go to varsity every day and try to read Dirac. I apply for fellowships abroad. But I can't really settle down to serious work, as Mike does. I know that I will leave Cape Town in a few months. I am restless.

Chapter 28
All the Leaves are Brown...
Separation Anxiety Redux

Having flirted with the idea of doing a PhD in America, at Cambridge, or at the Weizmann Institute in Israel, I decide on Columbia. Now I can give up studying until I get there, though I still go to varsity each weekday and take a few whacks at Dirac and a book on the mathematical theory of groups.

I have literally several scores of friends, from *Habonim* and from university, and I run around seeing them all as I prepare for my departure. Many tell me they are going to miss me and we make plans to write to each other until I come back for vacation after one year. But I feel squeezed by expectations of attachment, by the gravity they attribute to our relationship. I avoid serious conversations. I feel anxious. I freeze.

I begin to acquire all the things I will need in America. With my mother's help I pack them in two trunks that we will ship to New York. I fill them with clothes appropriate for a cold climate, books, old physics and maths notes, mementos. I am a sentimental person.

I spend a wonderfully distracted ten days working as a *Madrich* at a winter seminar camp for *Habonim* boys and girls of ten to twelve. It's a great relief to be busy all the time. I turn 21 there a month before my departure. At 11 pm, when the kids have gone to sleep, the other *Madrichim* give me a party with cakes and beer and bottles of champagne. At midnight, Raphie, whose parents are *landsleit* of mine, successively shakes each bottle, pops the cork, and sprays jets of champagne on everyone everywhere. We all get drunk. Some *Habonim* girls who are *Madrichot*[55] from the nearby seminar for older kids come over for my party. Late at night, after cleaning the room so that none of the children (or their parents) will know what happened, I drive the girls back to their seminar hotel. One of them, with whom I've had an attachment earlier, scolds me fiercely for being so stupid as to get drunk while looking after kids, and for driving drunk. I am woozy and know I am not driving well and try my best to conceal it. It doesn't take much to get me tipsy.

The remaining weeks are spent in preparation. I won't be back for a long time. I say goodbye to friends, to parents of friends, to professors and school teachers, to Dr Berelowitz. I drive by Mrs Azoulay's house but don't go in. I say goodbye to Mrs Gold whom I never see again. Her image stays with me, a kind of icon forever. I get vaccinations and an international driver's license. On July 31st I have a giant belated 21st birthday party at my sister Ruth's house in Sea Point. It's 1966 and we need dance music, so a friend and I spend Saturday afternoons for weeks listening to *Top Of The Pops* on Springbok Radio, recording three-minute hits on a reel-to-reel recorder. *All the leaves are brown, and the sky is gray ...*

The last few nights before I leave South Africa my parents have at-homes where anyone can drop in.

---

55 The feminine of *Madrichim*.

Uncles, aunts, cousins, friends come by. We take some last group photos.

I'm the last child at home. My parents will be alone now in the big empty house. I tell them they should join a sports club and take up lawn bowls for social life as many people their age do, but I know that it's not their style.

One last photo and the next morning I'm gone.

Photo Credits By Page Number

Page 1. Petrol pump, Alamy Stock Photo. B.O'Kane.

Page 2. Old telephone. James Steidl. Shutterstock.com

Page 2. Google Maps. 2023. 58 Salt River Road. Retrieved May 27, 2020.

Page 3. Photograph of Union Service Station. 1948. Author's personal collection.

Page 4. Green fence. Ongushi. Shutterstock.com.

Page 5. Photograph of author. 1947. Author's personal collection.

Page 6. Photograph of vinyl record. 1949. Author's personal collection.

Page 7. Photograph of author and his father. Approximately 1948. Author's personal collection.

Page 8. Photographs of author and his friend. Approximately 1950. Author's personal collection.

Page 10. Antique Print by J. H. Dowd. Approximately 1930. "If only I had two moufs!" Public domain. https://www.collector-sprints.com/303/antiqueprint/ifonlyihadtwomoufs

Page 11. Photograph of author's mother. Early 1930s. Author's personal collection.

Page 12. Photograph of author's parents wedding announcement. Early 1930s. Author's personal collection.

Page 13. Photograph of author's parents. Early 1930s. Author's personal collection.

Page 15. Top. Photograph of author's uncle and aunts. 1935. Author's personal collection.

Page 15. Middle. Photograph of author's uncle. Early 1930s. Author's personal collection.

Page 15. Bottom. Photograph of author's uncle. Early 1930s. Author's personal collection.

Page 17. Photograph of Tony Curtis. 1958. Public Domain.

Page 19. Apartheid beach sign. 6 July 1976. Keystone Press. Alamy Stock Photo.

Page 20. Union Service Station. 1940s. Author's personal collection.

Page 21. Top. Colored oil stain on the Asphalt. Andre K. Shutterstock.com.

Page 21. Middle. Diagram created by author.

Page 23. C/N 43157. SAAF 6904 Suit Afrikaanse Lugmag. South African Air Force Museum Swartkop Archives

Page 24. Miniature bananas. Author's personal collection.

Page 25. Middle. Sugar lollipop cockerel on white background. ALEXSTAND. Shutterstock.com.

Page 25. Bottom. Vintage Friction Spark Flint Toy Gun Made in Japan RARE Primitive. https://www.ebay.com/itm/295443410185/ eBay.

Page 27. General Jan Christiaan Smuts. Yousuf Karsh. 1943. Wikipedia. CC BY-SA 3.0.

Page 29. Author's kindergarten class. 1950. Author's personal collection,

Page 31. Author's ancestors. Author's personal collection.

Page 32. Author's father with friends. Early 1930s. Author's personal collection.

Page 33. Author's father's letterhead. Early 1950s. Author's personal collection.

Page 36. Author's parents' gravestones. Author's personal collection.

Page 37 Aerogramme. 1965. Author's personal collection.

Page 38. Car parked in front of author's home in Cape Town. 1964. Author's personal collection.

Page 39. Author's house in Cape Town. 1959. Author's personal collection.

Page 42. Garden of author's house in Cape Town. 1958. Author's personal collection.

Page 49. Bayko Building Set. Alamy Stock Photo. geogphotos

Page 50. Old Singer sewing machine. Emre Yen. Shutterstock.com.

Page 54. Sculpture of head of author by Mrs Josephson. 1955. Author's personal collection.

Page 57. Top. Liberace. Allen Warren. Wikipedia. CC-BY-SA 3.0.

Page 57. Middle. Loquats. Photo by Author. Author's personal collection.

Page 59. Middle Left. Brick Bradford's Time Top. Author's personal collection. Middle Right. Prince Valiant. Wikipedia. Public domain.

Page 60. Marbles. Author's personal collection.

Page 63. Bains Kloof Pass. Zaian. Wikipedia. Public domain.

Page 64. Enamelled metal chamberpot, British, 1901-1960. Science Museum Group Collection. The Board of Trustees of the Science Museum. Creative Commons 4 license. Public domain.

Page 73. If you see something. Public domain.

Page 77. Muizenberg. Public domain.

Page 78. The Snake Pit. Muizenberg. Public domain.

Page 82. Wicker basket with tableware for picnic on beige. Pixel-Shot. Shutterstock.com.

Page 83. Muizenberg beach and pavilion. Public domain.

Page 86. Middle. Yisroel Ben Menahem in Yard of Acre Prison. 1920. Author's personal collection.

Page 86. Bottom. Yisroel Ben Menahem in Acre Prison. 1920. Author's personal collection.

Page 87. Letter. Author's personal collection.

Page 88. Inscription in the Golden Book of the Jewish National Fund. Author's personal collection.

Page 89. Brooch. 1955. Author's personal collection.

Page 90. Tiger Comic. Public domain.

Page 91. Top. Girls' Crystal. Alamy Stock Photo. Retro AdArchives.

Page 91. Bottom. Pipe Track Cape Town. Flicker. CC 2 license.

Page 92. Quarry. Public domain.

Page 93. Top. Balsa plane. Public domain.

Page 93. Middle left. Cork cricket ball. Public domain.

Page 93. Middle right. A Shiny New Test Match Cricket Ball Leather Hard. HammadKhn.Shutterstock.com.

Page 94. Top. Antique wooden tennis racket vintage on white background. Supermop. Shutterstock.com.

Page 94. Middle. Dunlop Maxply tennis racket. Public domain.

Page 94. Bottom. Roger Bannister. Alamy Stock Photo. Zuma Press Inc. 4 June 1954.

Page 95. Molteno Dam from Belvedere Ave. 25 November 1910. Hilton Teper. Wikipedia. CC-BY-SA 3.0.

Page 96. Top. Ayuntamiento, Ciudad del Cabo, Sudàfrica. July 19 2018. Deigo Delso. Wikipedia. CC-BY-SA 4.0.

Page 96. Middle. Wrigley's P.K. Public domain.

Page 97. Vase with flowers. Author's personal collection.

Page 99. Eartha Kitt album. Public domain.

Page 100. Edinburgh Castle III (ship).jpg. 1948. Wikipedia. Public domain. Copyright expired.

Page 101. Amalia at the Paris Olympia. Public domain.

Page 102. The Negresco on the Promenade des Anglais in Nice. Public domain.

Page 105. Silhouette cutout. Author's personal collection.

Page 107. Bicester, Oxon, UK - Oct 9th 2022. 1965 black Morris Minor classic car driving on an English country road. Sue Thatcher. Shutterstock.com.

Page 108. Viceroy cigarette box. Public domain.

Page 109. Kelvin's Water Dropper. Thijs Knapen, "Analyzing and optimally controlling the Kelvin water dropper." (2015). https://essay.utwente.nl/68015/1/Knapen_MA_EEMCS.pdf

Page 110. Map of Africa with Zanzibar circled. United States Central Intelligence Agency. Map Division. (1950) Africa, Administrative Divisions. [Washington, D.C.: Central Intelligence Agency] [Map] Retrieved from the Library of Congress, https://www.loc.gov/item/97687633/.

Page 115. Dr Berelowitz. Author's personal collection.

Page 117. The Woman in Gold. Gustav Klimt, Public domain, via Wikimedia Commons.

Page 124. The Gardens Synagogue, Cape Town. Chris Snelling, CC-BY-SA 3.0 via Wikimedia Commons.

Page 127. Hermes. Oliver Denker. Alamy Stock Photo.

Page 128. Aerial view of Clifton beach. Lemaret Pierrick. Shutterstock.com.

Page 134. Textbook cover. Author's personal collection.

Page 135. Conway Stewart pen. Author's personal collection.

Page 136. Middle. From a 1915. U.S. Dept of Commerce Report. Public domain.

Page 137. Top. Wrapped parcel. Author's personal collection.

Page 137. Middle. Adderley St, Cape Town. Early 1950s. Public domain.

Page 139. Black Magic chocolate box. Public domain.

Page 140. Young men and women at a school dance. 1963. Author's personal collection.

Page 143. Scientology E-meter. 1960s. Public domain.

Page 144. Middle. Some *Habonim* group leaders. Early 1960s. Author's personal collection.

Page 148. At *Habonim* camp, working in the kitchen. Author's personal collection.

Page 155. Odalisque couchée aux magnolias. 1923. Henri Matisse. Public domain.

Page 156. The Syndics of the Clothmakers Guild. 1662. Rembrandt. Rijksmuseum, Amsterdam. Public domain.

Page 166. Nuclear resonance graph. Author's personal collection.

Page 168. Punched card program deck. 3 October 2006. Arnold Reinhold. Wikipedia. CC-BY-SA 3.0

Page 169. Collage by Author. 1967. Author's personal collection.

Page 173. Collins Diary 1966. Author's personal collection.

Page 178. Vinyl record, California Dreaming. Public domain.

Page 179. Bottom. Photo of author, parents, nephew. 1966. Author's personal collection.

Acknowledgments

I am very grateful to Beverly Bell for her editorial assistance and encouragement while this book was under way. With her fine eye for detail and firm but light touch, she was always available for one more read-through. I also thank Jim Grant and Paul Wilmott for reading the manuscript and offering helpful comments and encouragement. Ittamar Avin, Marcos Carreira, David Mandl and Stephen Pincus provided useful suggestions. I'm grateful for Nick Stone's elegant work in designing the book's layout and cover. Finally, from beginning to end and at every point along the way, I'm deeply indebted to Mark Buchanan and Ole Peters of London Mathematical Laboratory, who turned this project into a reality. Mark's constant and patient attention to detail, and his comments and suggestions and efforts over many months, drove it forward. Some names of real people and places in this memoir have been changed.

About the Author

Emanuel Derman is the author of *My Life as a Quant*, the 2004 memoir that first introduced the quant world to a wide audience. He is also the author of *Models.Behaving.Badly*, a meditation on the critical difference between models in the physical and social sciences. He is a frequent contributor to X/Twitter at @EmanuelDerman

Brief Hours and Weeks recalls a childhood and youth in Cape Town. The author likes the observation by Sheila Heti: "The self's report on itself is surely a great fiction."

Derman was born in South Africa but has spent most of his professional years in Manhattan in New York City, where he has made contributions to several fields. He started out as a theoretical physicist, doing research on unified theories of elementary particle interactions. At AT&T Bell Laboratories in the 1980s he developed programming languages for business modelling. From 1985 to 2002 he worked on Wall Street, running quantitative strategies research groups at Goldman Sachs, where he was appointed a managing director in 1997. The two financial models he developed there, the Black-Derman-Toy interest-rate model and the local volatility model, have become widely used industry standards. From 2003 to 2023 he was head of the Master's Program in Financial Engineering at Columbia, where he is now Professor Emeritus.

In both of his books Derman points out the dangers that inevitably accompany the use of models, which are merely limited metaphors that compare something you would like to understand with something similar, but not identical, that you *already* understand. He was named the IAFE Financial Engineer of the Year in 2000. He has a PhD in theoretical physics from Columbia University and is the author of numerous articles in elementary particle physics, computer science, and finance.

Printed in the USA
CPSIA information can be obtained
at www.ICGtesting.com
LVHW071211171124
796669LV00025B/13/J